GOD'S
Changing
ROOM

Step Into the Realm
Where God's Power
Transforms You!

Linn DeGennaro

Evergreen
PRESS

ISBN 1-58169-171-8
For Worldwide Distribution
Printed in the U.S.A.

Evergreen Press
P.O. Box 191540 • Mobile, AL 36619
800-367-8203

*Editor's Note: The names of the people mentioned in this book
have been changed to protect their privacy.*

Table of Contents

Dedication

To the memory of Ture, my father,

whose greatest joy was to tell others

about God's offer of a new life.

Acknowledgments

I acknowledge, first of all, my Lord and Savior, whose love

transforms ordinary people into extraordinary

men and women of God.

Thank you to all past and present who opened your hearts

to God's changing work. Your stories fill these

pages with hope and encouragement.

And thank you, Jim. You put your trust

in the Lord and took a

leap of faith.

Introduction

Our lives are full of change. Nature displays the process of growth in a myriad of forms and color. The human body constantly changes as it grows and matures. Society builds up and tears down its man-made structures at an amazing rate. Change also happens on the inside. A changing society and environment force us to adapt mentally and emotionally, as well as physically.

The most important changes happen in the human heart. Here lies the basis of all other changes—good and bad—for life's changes bring both negative and positive results. Positive change answers the need in all of us to grow, develop, and become part of something bigger and better than ourselves.

On our own, however, life's changes can overwhelm us, as if we were swimmers struggling against a dangerous current. Negative changes can take us farther and farther from our goals for a successful and productive life.

Two thousand years ago, God opened the way for a new current of godly power to flow to His people. A new wave of inner sincerity and truth flows into our lives as God adds His strength to ours. God's change brings inner growth. Hope lives in our hearts instead of resentment; faith builds instead of fear; patience overcomes anger; and love wins out over bitterness. A healthy lifestyle takes shape as continued change opens more of our lives to God's power. Accomplishments build along with a sense of satisfaction as God fills our lives with His presence.

God's life-changing work culminates in a change in behavior. Others notice that you and I speak and act differently. A new personality emerges—a personality that is like us and yet somehow more than us—strong, yet kind and gentle with God's love.

The wave of good and lasting change crests. We do new things for God as we ride wave after wave of positive change toward God's shore of success. His love matures us into new people with a new purpose. We serve Him and achieve more lasting happiness than we ever thought possible.

The life of good and godly change begins in a moment of time with a single act of faith. God calls everyone by His love into a new current of positive change. He adds His strength to ours. We ride out the waves of negative change and swim toward shore with skillful and powerful strokes. The past becomes only a memory. The future comes alive in our hearts. The best and highest this life has to offer opens up to us.

God's loving touch on our spirits changes us forever.

Chapter 1

Faith: Practice Makes Perfect

God brings change into our lives through faith. He helps us build our faith as we practice on the small problems of everyday life. God meets one day's need. Then He meets the next day's need. Our faith builds one day at a time.

Practicing faith is like putting small, but manageable, deposits into an account of trust in God. Soon we have a large deposit of faith funds available for immediate withdrawal.

━━◆◆━━

Diane began practicing her faith right after the divorce. After 20 years of marriage, divorce was a bumpy road to travel. But when she started looking to God for help, she didn't feel so alone.

Diane kept turning to the Lord in the details of her daily life. One day as she sat in line at the inspection station, Diane closed her eyes and said a silent prayer, asking God to help her car pass inspection. She really needed it to pass because there was no money or time if it didn't. It was the end of the month.

Twenty minutes later, Diane drove out of the inspection

station with a brand-new "passed" sticker on her windshield. Her car had sailed right through. Thank You, God! For the first time in awhile, she thought she might be on the right road after all.

Diane felt a sense of comfort, knowing that God cared about even the little things in her life. She asked for God's help with her emotional struggles and prayed for her grandchild to do well in school. Even when God didn't respond immediately, she still trusted Him. Without realizing it, Diane was developing a relationship of trust with God. She was building up quite a large deposit of available, working faith.

The day came when the doctor found a lump in Diane's breast. He scheduled her for a test at the hospital to confirm his findings. A few days later, the scan did confirm the presence of a large lump. Although everyone used the words "probably benign" and attached various favorable percentages to her situation, the doctor told Diane the lump definitely needed to be removed. He scheduled Diane for outpatient surgery three-and-a-half weeks later.

Diane knew she had to ask God for His help. Because Diane had practiced her faith over a period of time, she had developed quite a habit of going to God for help. She already believed He would help her through the surgery and make sure she healed completely afterwards. She also prayed about the lump, asking that it would indeed be benign.

The day of her surgery arrived, and strange things happened at the hospital. The technician did a new scan to pinpoint the location of the lump so that the doctor could perform the surgery. Unbeknownst to Diane, the lump did not show up on the new scan. Startled and confused, the doctor compared the new scan to the one taken three weeks earlier, and then ordered a second scan. No lump. But the doctor was persistent. He called in another doctor to read yet a third scan. Still no lump.

Meanwhile, in the operating room, Diane waited for the doctor to come in and begin the procedure. She wondered what was taking so long. There was no explanation from the technicians, but they looked a bit upset about something. Afraid to ask if anything was wrong, Diane waited and wondered through two more scans. Finally, one technician came in and told her to get dressed and come into the conference room.

The technicians and the doctor explained the delay. They couldn't find the lump that had been there three weeks before, and they had no solution to the case of the missing lump. They were even apologetic. "We don't know what happened. We just can't explain it. You can go home because there is no reason to do the surgery. You just need to come back in a year for a follow-up test. But today we can't find any trace of the lump."

Diane's joy began as a warm glow on the inside. It spread rapidly through her body with a wave of happiness. She almost leaped out of her chair. A miracle! A real, live miracle! This was more than she had prayed for. The news of God's love was too good to keep to herself. She could not resist telling the doctor what had happened to the lump. God had healed her supernaturally. She felt as if her feet barely touched the floor when she left the hospital that day.

Diane's faith practice brought a perfect result. Practicing her faith on a regular basis built it into a great faith, a faith that could handle any crisis.

——◈◈——

A great faith starts out small, like the grain of mustard seed Jesus talked about. But the more we practice, the more our faith develops. Developing faith changes us. It opens the door to a more positive attitude toward life. We speak more optimistic words. And finally, faith affects our behavior. It stabilizes us because we become convinced of God's trustworthiness.

Faith, like all eternal substances, is invisible to our natural eyes. As God meets need after need, we begin to "see" our faith at work. God gives us a visible track record of faith's results on which we can look back.

———※·◦·※———

A story in ancient Israel shows us how a widow's developing faith paid an extraordinary dividend.

The widow in question lived around 800 B.C. Before her husband died, he had been a theological student at the school run by the prophet Elisha. At these types of schools, in existence for more than 200 years, the men studied what would amount to a seminary course today leading to ordination. This widow found herself in a worst-case scenario, the harshest and bumpiest of roads that godly change could take for a woman of her day. Her husband was a man of God, but he died leaving her penniless, with only two boys and a huge debt. Without insurance, Social Security, or even food stamps, the prophet's widow was helpless. The only choice left to her was to watch the creditors come and take her sons to sell into slavery.

In 2 Kings 4:1-7, the widow went to Elisha and presented her desperate situation. When the prophet asked what she had left in the house, her penniless plight was revealed in her answer: "Thine handmaid hath nothing in the house, save a pot [small jar] of oil." Elisha told her to borrow as many jars, pots and other vessels to hold oil as she could, and then close herself and her sons in the house and pour out the oil from the small pot into the borrowed containers.

This brave and faithful woman knew something about God. She had trusted Him enough to go to His prophet, much as we would go to a pastor today. Her husband had been a prophet himself and may have gone into debt to support his family while studying at the prophets' school. She likely had supported him in his endeavor to serve God.

I believe that Elisha told this woman to borrow as many empty oil containers as she could for a spiritual reason as well as a practical reason. These containers were not just to hold the oil, but also to give the widow practice in using her faith. Her miracle actually started when the widow put her faith to work by asking a nearby neighbor for the first borrowed jar. When she got to the third or fourth neighbor and received more borrowed containers, her faith began to build. By the time she reached the other side of town, she began to get excited as her sons took the jars from her and brought them home to put with the others. I believe all of their faith developed into greatness as they collected jar after jar. Probably the three of them went to other families whose men attended the schools of the prophets and collected as many vessels as they could.

The empty house filled with so many containers that she and her sons had to stack them everywhere: on the table, on the floor, and on the shelves. There were so many containers that they may have even been tripping over the jars- and each other! By the time the widow shut the door on the three of them and the jars, I believe the faith in the household had already developed into a great level of anticipation. *Their faith multiplied before the oil multiplied.*

How the three of them must have rejoiced when the first container filled to the brim from her small pot! As her first son put that jar carefully to the side, the younger brother carried an empty vessel to his mother. Then that one filled, and another, and another. The widow concentrated on her pouring as the boys carried vessel after vessel to her, carefully setting aside each full one. She didn't even realize she had filled the last vessel until her son told her there were no more empty ones. And that is when the oil stopped flowing.

The widow and her sons would never forget the day the oil multiplied. Faith could not bring their husband and father back, but through their faith, God saved them from poverty and delivered the sons from a life of slavery. Due to the high value of oil in those days, the widow could sell it at a good price, pay her family's debt, and have enough left over to support herself and her sons.

Each day presents us with a new opportunity to practice our faith. Today we practice our faith on today's concerns, while tomorrow's needs bring further opportunities to build our faith.

Our faith practice brings perfect results. Diane's small daily deposits of faith paid a miraculous dividend of healing. And God supernaturally provided for the widow and her two sons through their multiplying faith.

A practicing faith becomes a powerful force for good and godly change. It is God's doorway to improvement in our lives. It allows God to enter relationships and alter circumstances, all in a good and positive way.

God builds our faith into a great faith, a faith that changes lives. *God's Changing Room* gives us faith practice, and practice makes our faith perfect.

Chapter 2

Foundational Change

God created each of us with a basic blueprint, a personality fitted to our individual nature and yet patterned after Him. During growth from infancy to adulthood, you and I made alterations to God's original plan. Outside influences also affected our development. The resulting personality structure contains a combination of strengths and weaknesses.

When each of us comes to God in life-changing faith, our whole personality structure undergoes a major change. God sets this structure of our basic nature, the heart, on the foundation of His eternal nature. His strength gives stability to the house of our heart and soul and allows us to overcome our weaknesses.

———⊷⊶———

Ron found himself looking back to the foundation of faith he knew as a child. At that time, he believed in God with a child's simple faith, but his teenage years were ones of rebellion and hurt as he watched his parents' marriage end in divorce. A year ago, something happened that made him look back. His wife, Marcia, was sick with a serious infection and admitted to the hospital. The doctors prescribed medication, but it was only after family and friends started praying for her that she began to improve. Now she was well, and they wanted to start a family. Was what he believed as a child true after all?

Ron wanted to build on something solid for the future. The land, he thought, was like God: solid, something a man could come back to time after time. Ron and Marcia finally had that land. All the acres where he now stood belonged to them. Straight ahead, just over the hill, was state forest land. To the right were the woods, and to the left was the lake. He and Marcia wanted to raise their children here. He stood on the spot where they planned to build their house. He could picture it now. It would be a saltbox style with white siding.

A cold blast of February wind brought him back to the present. There were new problems with the construction of the house. The township said they needed a variance from the zoning code to start construction. The legal process involved lawyers, architects and all kinds of forms and fees. It was long, and it was expensive. Ron began to wonder which would give out first—their money or the local governing board.

Ron finished staking the location of the house in the semi-darkness and drove home tired from a full day's work at the office. He found Marcia at the kitchen table struggling with a new three-page letter from the township detailing 11 objections to their proposed building plans. They had to answer all 11 points at the meeting on Thursday night. Worse yet, a message on the answering machine said their attorney could not make the meeting and was sending a new lawyer in his place. It was already Monday, and they had to get all this information to the new lawyer before the meeting.

As more discouragement began to settle over them both, Marcia suggested calling Mary, her aunt. Mary was active in real estate and could give them advice. She advised them not to give up and to make sure the lawyer had all the information before the meeting. Then she told them that her next calls would be to her church prayer chain and family members who regularly prayed for others. They would all agree in prayer for God's help on Thursday night.

Ron again thought back to his childhood foundation of faith. Was God's love the bedrock of a good future? Could Ron still build a future on God's Son and His love? Ron hoped this was true, because he definitely needed a miracle at Thursday night's meeting. The past committee meetings he and Marcia had attended were lengthy, with one question after another wearing them down. Getting the majority to agree to their plan on all 11 issues seemed impossible.

The night of the meeting came quickly. On the way in, the new lawyer told them that he had reviewed the information and thought they needed a fair amount of time to address all the issues. In his presentation, he planned to give the committee ample time to discuss each point thoroughly. The most he expected was that the committee would postpone the decision.

The meeting started well with the lawyer's opening remarks. He covered the first point and the second and got all the way through point number five before one committee member even raised a question. The next page of objections also went quickly, with another committee member agreeing out loud with their suggested answer to point number seven. When they hit the top of the third page, nearing the end of the list, Ron and Marcia were almost afraid to hope. The next-to-last point concerned the road to be built onto the property, and Ron agreed to the committee's suggestion for its location-and then they were on the last point. Two people raised questions and then said they were satisfied with the entire plan. The committee agreed and unanimously gave permission for construction to begin. The resolution for the variance would be formalized at the next meeting.

The next thing Ron and Marcia knew, they were walking out of the meeting smiling and laughing and shaking hands with everyone. The lawyer seemed especially pleased as he congratulated them. Then they were in the car on the way home rejoicing. Marcia was crying for joy, and Ron was saying it was a miracle. They called Mary from the car. "We got it! We got it!" They were so excited she could hardly understand their words. Then Ron thanked her for her prayers and asked her to thank everyone else who had prayed for them. He repeated, "It was like a miracle."

Marcia and Ron paid a visit to their land the next day. Together they took in the view over the lake. Ron knew things would come up in the future for which he would need God's help. That was okay, though, because he was already building on God's stable foundation of love and truth.

God rebuilds the house of our heart from the ground up, because He knows the most important changes are the basic changes we must make in character and attitude. He builds His strengths into our lives as His Spirit oversees a step-by-step process of tearing down the old and building up the new. God's Spirit removes the decaying wood of human weakness from the heart and adds new timbers of godly strength.

God knocks on the door of every heart whose structure

is in need of repair. He wants to help His people get their spiritual house in order.

———◆———

Even in A.D. 33, people needed to lay a godly foundation for their lives. First, however, they needed to recognize that they had previously built their house on a shaky one.

Zaccheus studied his tax rolls in his office in Jericho. *I must be getting soft*, he told himself. The last man could have paid more than he did, but his six children awoke a sense of compassion in Zaccheus. He would make less this quarter than usual. *But I have more than enough already*, he thought, *more than I can spend . . .* He caught himself. *Yes, I must be getting soft*.

Zaccheus did what most tax collectors did in those days. He collected more taxes than the Romans actually required and kept the extra. Lately, however, a sense of responsibility toward God and man had awakened within him, and he was finding it difficult to demand his usual amount.

As a young man, Zaccheus used to worship on the high holy days in the Temple. He remembered the services and the sacrificial altar. He had often felt a sense of awe, as if he had actually been in God's presence. He remembered the prophecies he had heard then about the Messiah coming to save His people. He often dreamed about it and hoped he would have a chance to meet the Messiah if He came during Zaccheus's lifetime. As he grew older, those memories faded in the face of his need to earn a living. Without a real trade to speak of, he turned to tax collecting as a last resort. A growing need for money weakened his sense of responsibility toward God and his fellow men. His promotion to chief tax collector eroded what was left of his conscience, and Zaccheus developed hardheartedness toward his own race. With Roman taxes on everything from produce, land, items bought and sold, and export and import customs paid at the city gate, Zaccheus soon amassed a small fortune.

Lately, however, he had begun to hear stories about a miracle-working Rabbi who healed everyone who came to Him, even lepers. The blind received their sight, the deaf heard, and the lame walked again. Could these stories be responsible for reawakening Zaccheus's conscience? What if this Rabbi was God's anointed? "God," he prayed aloud, "if You allow me to see Him, and He is the Messiah, I'll give You half of my wealth." *I really am getting soft,* Zaccheus thought to himself, *or maybe I'm more of a son of Abraham than I thought.*

One day early in the spring, Zaccheus learned that the Rabbi had entered the city gate. *Maybe God is answering my prayer,* Zaccheus thought and rushed out into the street. He started toward the gate, but the street was mobbed with people trying to get near the Rabbi. Zaccheus pushed and shoved but could not get close enough to get a good look. *All I want to do is see Him,* he thought. This was one of those times he hated being as short as he was. He strained his neck and struggled to see into the street.

The Rabbi was passing by, and Zaccheus was going to miss out on it all. He clenched his fists in frustration when suddenly the idea hit him. He ran ahead of the crowd and down the street. One block, two blocks, and the crowd thinned out a little, but Zaccheus still could not see. Repeatedly he kept weaving in and out of the crowd, trying to get a good look. The noise told him that the Rabbi was approaching. In his excitement, he bumped into the tree, giving him a terrific idea. He had just enough time so he quickly began to climb. Desperation drove him upward and out onto the lowest limb overlooking the street. He crouched down holding onto some smaller branches, eyes fixed on the street below.

There He was, the Rabbi, coming closer and closer in the midst of His followers. Zaccheus could not take his eyes off Him. There was a sense of God's presence about Him that Zaccheus recognized from the Temple services. The Rabbi came right under Zaccheus's tree and stopped. He looked up as if He knew Zaccheus was there. Their eyes met. Something in Zaccheus's heart came alive as the Rabbi called up to him, "Zaccheus, hurry and come down from there. I have to stay at your house today."

The Rabbi's followers and many guests dined at Zaccheus's house that evening. The Rabbi spoke to individuals and to the group as a whole. He even spoke to Zaccheus as if they were old friends, and Zaccheus welcomed the Rabbi as his Messiah and treated Him as royalty. Early in the evening Zaccheus remembered his responsibility before God. A promise was a promise. Zaccheus rose to his feet before the Rabbi and all who were present and spoke what was in his heart: "Lord, today I promise to give half of what I own to the poor." The next words came out before he even realized it: "And if I have assessed taxes on anyone falsely, I pledge to restore it to them four times over." Zaccheus sat down to stunned silence.

The Rabbi accepted Zaccheus in front of everyone, calling him a "son of Abraham." "A lasting and permanent change," He said, came to Zaccheus's physical house and to the dwelling place of his heart. Zaccheus's heart and house now rested on God's strength, and the rotten wood of greed was replaced by the support beam of a good conscience toward God and man.

Today the Messiah works in each heart and soul who welcomes His rebuilding process. He keeps each individual personality intact, yet He expands and develops the mind and heart into a home for His Spirit. His construction project builds a new house on His foundation, beginning with good changes in character and attitude. As we continue in the life of good and godly change, the Messiah's perfect building materials make us over into new people. Like Ron, we learn to rest our hopes on the solid foundation of God's love. Or like Zaccheus, we build on the attitude of commitment toward God and compassion toward others.

God's Changing Room lays the groundwork for a better life. Life is different because we are different. We live a new life, a life that brings us peace and joy.

Chapter 3

The Power of Choice

Change challenges our faith because it opens the door to the unknown. God brings new benefits into our lives through change. He gives us advantages that are unavailable in our current situation.

God never forces His people to change. Whether the change needs to occur in the small things of daily life or involves a major life decision, God gives us the power to choose whether or not to make the change. Larry needed to make a major life decision, but God left the acceptance of the change in Larry's hands.

———

Larry looked at the clock in his office again. It couldn't be only 1:15 in the afternoon. He had been working since 9 a.m. and had never seen a day drag so slowly. There had been a time when there weren't enough hours in a day, but that was years ago when he started the business. He began the company 20 years ago on a shoestring and had watched it grow into one of the largest suppliers of gardening equipment on the East Coast. Three years ago, he offered to retire and leave the business to his son, Steve. Larry then planned to cut back on his days in the office and leave the day-to-day operations of the business in Steve's hands. When he tried to take a day off, however, he found himself worrying. *What if something should go wrong? What if Steve made the wrong decision? What if it hurt the company finan-cially?* Larry was concerned about living on a retirement income and worried that the company might not be able to support both Steve and himself in the future. Overall, he was growing more irritable and losing his ability to get along with people.

The intercom buzzed. Steve said he needed to see Larry immediately. When Steve came in, he looked upset, and Larry tensed in response. Steve announced that they had just lost another account. It seemed that Larry had promised this account a delivery by a certain date, but not only did the shipment not arrive, the order had never been put on the production and delivery schedules. They couldn't even promise the account a late delivery. Larry tried to defend the indefensible without admitting he had just plain forgotten about the order. But Steve became angry, declaring that this was the third time this had happened in as many months. Tension rose along with the anger in their voices. Steve said he was tired of waiting for his father to keep his promise to retire, accusing Larry of having too much of his identity locked up in the business. Larry accused Steve of trying to force him out. Steve left, slamming the door behind him.

Larry sat down, upset with himself. Steve was right. His son had the college education and years of experience in the business as he prepared for the day his father would retire.

Whose side am I on? Larry wondered. Sometimes it seemed he was working for the competition. He was forgetting too many important things lately, and he was constantly saying things for which he later had to apologize. This was one of those times.

Larry went into Steve's office and tried to smooth things over yet another time. But Steve stood firm. He said the business was being hurt by two people being in charge and pulling it in two different directions. Employee morale was sinking, and the business would soon be in financial trouble if the situation continued. Steve offered his father a year's pay as a consultant if he would stick to their original agreement and let his son take over the day-to-day operation of the business. For the sake of the business, Steve was asking his father to back out. When Larry refused, Steve reluctantly made a hard decision. "Then I'll go," he said. "At this rate, neither one of us is helping the company." And Steve left, sadly but quietly.

The next morning Larry went to talk to his pastor. They discussed the situation at length, especially Steve's accusation that Larry was putting the company in danger by not letting go. The pastor explained a paradoxical truth. Larry was holding onto his life in the business, afraid that letting go would mean a loss of identity, financial resources, and even the business itself. But in actuality, his holding onto something he had outgrown could cost him the very losses he was trying to avoid. By holding onto his current position, the stress was causing him to lose the ability to get along with people. His behavior was costing the company many business accounts and negatively impacting employee morale.

The pastor shared with him that if Larry chose to accept this change and let go of his position, he might have to give up some things. God, however, would not leave empty places in his life for long. He would fill Larry's life with good things, new benefits to take the place of the old benefits he once enjoyed. The pastor encouraged Larry to pray and seek God's will, to reverse his attitude from one of resisting change to acceptance.

Larry decided to talk with Nancy, his wife, about lifestyle changes they could make in order to live on a retirement income. That evening, he and Nancy discussed selling their extra properties and keeping the one house they really needed. Nancy's response surprised him. She said she was willing to make a trade. She wanted to visit their grandchildren who lived out West more often. She also reminded him that they had neglected their joint hobby of playing golf the last few years, and she wanted to take that up again and spend more time together. These things were more important than an extra home, cars, and a vacation cottage.

The next morning, Larry accepted Steve's offer to stay on as consultant for a year. That would give him time to consolidate some of his property and reduce his living expenses. He would cut down his days in the office to two a week, and eventually to zero as he turned over the remainder of the day-to-day operations to Steve.

Steve thanked his father for his acceptance of the consulting offer. To his surprise, Larry then went on to say that he was taking the rest of the day off to play golf and would see his son tomorrow, and then Larry turned and walked out the door.

Two years later, Larry continues to enjoy his retirement. During the first year, he made the necessary changes to become financially free to retire. He learned to let go of the reins in the business by giving Steve the freedom to make a mistake. Certainly he had made his own share of mistakes during the time he built the business. The more he stepped back and trusted God, the more his anxieties faded.

More importantly, Larry established his connection with God as his number-one priority. He regained his peace of mind and his ability to enjoy being with people. Prayer gave him the strength to keep his thoughts heading in a positive, life-affirming direction. Freed from a nine-to-five routine, each day now brings Larry the enjoyment of new things. Sometimes it is visiting his grandchildren. Sometimes it is volunteering at a nearby rehabilitation center. Other times it is playing golf with Nancy. Larry let go of the old, and God reached down and filled the empty places in his life with good things, giving Larry a sense of appreciation for His many good gifts.

Change is a part of life. In the past, change has often led us in the wrong direction, and the unknown seemed to hold negative things for us. As a result, you and I can find ourselves fearing what lies around the next bend and hesitating when confronting the unfamiliar. We resist taking a step forward into the new things God has for us.

Today's changes are different when God goes ahead of us. He prepares the way and gives us the guidance and direction we need to be ready for the next change. His strength supports us through the adjustment period and propels us into the time of enjoying the benefits.

The Bible tells of a woman who embraced a major life change. She followed God's lead and found herself in the right place at the right time.

Ruth lived during a lawless time, a period in Israel's history when "every man did what was right in his own eyes." She married Mahlon, a Jewish man, who lived in her country of Moab. Mahlon and his brother died over the next several years, leaving only the women of the household— Naomi, Ruth's mother-in-law; Orpah, her sister-in-law; and Ruth. Naomi decided to return to her hometown of Bethlehem in the land of Israel. She told her daughters-in-law to stay in Moab, return to their families, and marry again. Both young women wept bitterly at the thought of leaving her, and all three started out on foot on the trip to Bethlehem.

A short distance into the 120-mile journey that would take them across the mountains and into the land of Israel, Naomi again urged both daughters-in-law to return to their families. Orpah, weeping, turned back toward her homeland. But Ruth told Naomi that she would never leave her: "Thy people shall be my people and thy God, my God." Both young women had affection for Naomi, but Ruth also had faith in Naomi's God, the God of Israel. Ruth followed her faith into a strange land and left everything familiar behind—home, country, language, religion and culture.

The moment Ruth declared her faith in the God of Israel, she could let go of the old. When she did, the door to God's future swung wide open. In the days and weeks ahead, Ruth would find herself in the right place at the right time to walk boldly through that door into her new future.

Naomi and Ruth arrived in Bethlehem at the time of the fall harvest. Naomi's old friends and neighbors learned about her changed circumstances. She had left 10 years before with a husband and two sons. Now she had returned, alone except for Ruth, whose loyalty and love would soon earn the praise of everyone who knew her.

Naomi and Ruth faced a bleak future. Without a man to support them, they were very poor and lacked even the basic necessities of life. In 1100 B.C., Israel had only one social safety net. It was called "gleaning." Under Mosaic Law, farmers had to leave the corners of their fields unharvested. They also had to leave leftover sheaves of grain where they fell. The poor would follow along after the harvesters and pick up any grain that was left in the field. In theory, gleaning provided food for the poor. In practice, it exposed a lone woman to danger in the fields from male workers.

Nevertheless, the need for food forced Ruth into this system. The first morning Ruth set out to glean, she picked a field at random and worked through most of the morning gathering the grain that fell from the harvesters' baskets and wagon. The owner of the field, a wealthy man named Boaz, arrived to check on the work. He noticed the attractive young woman gleaning behind his workers, and the stage was set for the unfolding of God's perfect plan.

Their first meeting had all the earmarks of love at first sight as acted out in an ancient near-Eastern culture. Boaz's initial thought was to protect Ruth. He told her to stay in his field near his workers where she would be safe. She thanked him deeply for what she realized was a special favor in light of her status as a foreigner. He told her he knew something about her heart and her courage in leaving her home and caring for her mother-in-law in a strange land. He also knew that she and he now worshiped the same God, the Lord God of Israel. She acknowledged the kindness of the godly man who would take the time to encourage a young widow on her difficult and lonely path.

Boaz invited Ruth to eat the noontime meal with his regular workers, and afterward he ordered the reapers to let her work undisturbed and to let some grain fall on purpose in her path.

When Ruth arrived home with more than a bushel of grain, Naomi asked her whose field she had worked in. As she shared the leftover portion of her noontime meal, Ruth told Naomi all the details. Naomi's heart filled with wonder and hope. Boaz was a member of her husband's extended family. According to the custom of the time, he could act as a kinsman-redeemer and claim Ruth's hand in marriage. Ruth's son by Boaz would carry Mahlon's name. In fact, Ruth even had a legal right to approach Boaz and ask him to take her as his wife to carry on this custom.

This happy solution (which would have provided for Naomi, as well) did not materialize. Ruth worked every day in Boaz's field for several months as Naomi and she lived on the grain she collected from the barley and wheat harvests. During this time, Boaz continued to provide for and protect Ruth, while Ruth turned down several other suitors. Perhaps Boaz's concern over his age (he was 20 or more years Ruth's senior) kept him from approaching Ruth, and Ruth's shyness and nationality kept her from going to him. This unhappy state of affairs could have continued indefinitely if Naomi hadn't intervened.

Naomi wanted a good future for her young, attractive and gentle-spirited daughter-in-law. She saw the obvious—two people in love—and fashioned a bold plan to bring this situation to a conclusion.

The night Boaz celebrated the barley harvest, Naomi told Ruth to bathe and perfume herself and dress in her best outfit. She told Ruth to go to the threshing floor and hide herself until Boaz had eaten and drunk. Boaz celebrated with his workers and then lay down to sleep near the pile of grain in order to guard it. Ruth slipped out of hiding, and quietly lay down at his feet, covering herself with his blanket. Trusting in his honorable character, she came as close to the position of a wife as she could without compromising her own virtue.

After midnight, Boaz awoke and discovered a woman lying at his feet. "Who is it?" he called into the darkness. "I am Ruth, your servant." Boldly, Ruth placed her legal claim to his protection before him. "Lift me to your side as your wife. You have the right of kinship to redeem all that belongs to me."

Her request delighted his heart, for it told him that she turned down other suitors because she had waited for him. It told him that his age did not matter to her. It told him that his feelings were returned, that the heart of the lovely young woman at his feet belonged to him.

Unfortunately, there was another family member who was closer in relation, and he could claim Ruth ahead of Boaz. Boaz needed to resolve this issue, and he promised to do so as soon as daylight came. Ruth waited until just before dawn and left the threshing floor while Boaz again protected her reputation by ordering his workers to keep secret that a woman had come that night to the threshing floor.

The next day, Boaz removed the last obstacle between them. The man who was next of kin refused to marry Ruth because her child would become heir to all of his estate. He could not put his family's inheritance in jeopardy. Then Boaz declared his intention to take Ruth as his wife in front of the town elders.

The story ends as Ruth marries Boaz and receives wealth instead of poverty. Ruth gave birth to a son named Obed and made Naomi a grandmother. Obed became the grandfather of King David, the royal line through which God would bring the Savior into the world. The Bible gives Ruth a place of honor as one of the ancestors of Jesus Christ, one of the few women listed in an all-male genealogy.

Larry chose to let go of the old and the known in order to take hold of a new, unknown future. Ruth left behind all that was familiar to embrace God's plan. Just as it worked for Larry and Ruth, it works for us, too. Letting go of the old frees our hearts from fear and gives us the power of choice. Courage replaces fear as we realize the unknown is unknown only to us. The future is always known to God. It is just as likely to hold good things as bad.

Once we choose to change, the rest is much easier. God goes ahead of us and opens the door to the future. Choosing a forward step empowers us. Holding back weakens us. Accelerated growth occurs with an attitude of openness and acceptance of new things. *God's Changing Room* brings the future into the now. Good things are waiting for us.

Chapter 4

The Past in Perspective

After we come to God in life-changing faith, a new understanding tugs at our spirits. The past comes into perspective as we recognize God's hand in our lives. We become aware of a guiding and protective influence that has been with us for a long time.

Distant and faraway memories become clear, silhouetted against the harsh backdrop of danger.

———

A faded memory came to the forefront of Jim's mind as he sat one morning reading his new Bible. Several weeks ago, his life changed with an act of faith. He opened his heart to the God he had denied for so long, and God changed him. The despair over his broken marriage lifted. Already his life started to change for the better. In fact, he had just met someone new, someone who believed in God as he did. The future looked brighter, and he hoped it held some positive changes in the area of relationships.

Jim knew that in order for these good changes to continue, he had to change, as well. He obeyed the urgings of his spirit and got up early each day to partake of some spiritual food for thought along with his physical breakfast. To his surprise, he enjoyed it. Reading the New Testament was a first for him. He found the Lord's Prayer in the book of Matthew, as well as the Golden Rule. *So that is where we get expressions like "salt of the earth" and a "mustard seed of faith,"* Jim realized. He learned that God's ways are different than man's. God is concerned with motive, not with social prestige or outward show.

God promised to care for Jim. God held power over the whole earth, and yet He promised to stay with Jim, even as far as the end of the world and as long as the end of time. Did that mean all through the time of Jim's life? Did that mean God was with Jim even before he came to a place of faith in God?

Jim closed the Bible and shut his eyes. He remembered another time of terrible danger and another place at the other end of the world.

From the safety of his kitchen, Jim looked back almost 30 years. It was nighttime. In his mind's eye, he saw a flash of light as a rocket arced across the black jungle sky. He was 400 meters from the Cambodian border, west of Saigon. He remembered it all as if it had happened only last week.

All started out quiet that night on the firebase. Jim came on duty at 11 p.m. in the tactical operations center in the main bunker. A few minutes later, the sergeant went to his adjoining bunker and said, "Going to sleep. See you in the morning." The rocket continued its deadly arc over the perimeter of the base, coming straight on course for the bunker. It hit the sergeant's bunker dead center. The explosion blew out the front wall of the command bunker and blasted the sergeant's body through his bunker's solid wall of ammo crates and sandbags. At that moment, the night sky lit up with machine guns and heavy artillery fire, as every gun in the base fired in retaliation at the unseen enemy. The enemy, now discovered, fired back with everything they had. The noise was deafening, and the sky crisscrossed with tracers, artillery and machine-gun fire. It was like the Fourth of July gone crazy.

The light and the noise freeze-framed that night in Jim's memory. They found the sergeant's body outside the bunker in the mud. He was alive, but badly injured. As Jim administered first aid, his efforts seemed pathetic. The sergeant had gashes under both eyes and a torn scalp, internal bleeding from a ruptured spleen and a foot almost severed from the explosion. They radioed for help and called for a chopper for the wounded man. The damaged front wall of the bunker left them exposed, like bait in a trap. Any minute the enemy could reach them, or another rocket could finish what the first one had started. Fear on the ground added to the confusion overhead.

The battle raged around and over them. Fear, adrenaline, and overwhelming noise and light against the dark jungle night gave it all a super-charged reality. Every second seemed locked in time as they brought the sergeant outside the bunker perimeter to the landing pad-all under heavy enemy fire and waited for the helicopter. Jim never heard what happened to the sergeant. He hoped—really hoped— that the man had made it.

Months passed. Many nights later, Jim came home from Vietnam physically whole, but mentally and emotionally scarred. He felt relief and even guilt at making it home while so many others did not. He felt anger over his lost youth and innocence and the missing years taken out of his life. For a time, he rebelled against society, the government, life in general, and even God. The one thing he never did was thank God for bringing him home safely and in one piece.

Even after he came home from the war, Jim came to depend on a streetwise sense of intuition, an inner voice that warned him many times of impending danger. Now he recognized the Source of that voice. God had watched over Jim for many years until he came to God in an act of faith. Now he realized just how much he owed God. He owed Him his life—a hundred times over.

———

God brings our thinking into the present by putting the past in perspective. Each of us has his or her own individual history with God, times when we felt His influence or followed His guidance without being aware of who was helping us. God wants to lead us forward in the life of good and godly change, but before He does, He needs to take us back a step or two. It is important that we know the truth. It is essential that the past lose its hold over us.

———

The New Testament tells the story of a young man who needed to put the past in perspective. God let him go his own way when he wanted to, but God still watched over him. At a critical turning point, He influenced the young man to come back home to the good life—the life of godly changes, growth, and development.

The young man shouldered his pack and walked a little faster after his rest. Every few minutes, his hand went to his money belt and checked the bulge and weight of it to make sure all the contents were there. It represented his fortune—one-third of his father's vast estate—his total inheritance. According to Jewish law, his older brother was to get twice as much. At the memory of his brother, his fist clenched, and he walked even faster, trying to put as much distance as possible between him and his home. His brother was always throwing in his face how much he did around the farm and the vineyard. His brother hung out with his friends who were just like him: all work and no play. Hypocrites! For all their "religion," he often saw them treating the servants and workers cruelly. And his father never seemed to see through their act. Such a phony, joyless existence was not for him. He wanted some real fun out of life.

He traveled until he came to a resort area and stayed at the best hotel. His fast lifestyle and easy money soon attracted friends—both men and women—who flattered him while living off his reckless generosity. Sooner, rather than later, the money ran out. So did his new "friends." At that time, a deep economic recession hit the resort's tourism industry. Work was impossible to find, so he signed on with a corporation that managed a large farm. He soon regretted his move. He and the other workers were treated almost like slaves. They were beaten often and ill-fed. Even the pig feed began to look good to him. Filthy, starving, and ragged, he feared for his life. It was only a matter of time until illness would claim his remaining strength.

Hunger pangs forced him to his senses. Although he had been born into the privileged position of a son, his father's servants were now better off than he was. How he must have hurt his father. All this time, and he had never even sent word home that he was alive. After the way he behaved, he wouldn't blame his father if he were disowned. But he decided to go home anyway and beg his father to have pity on him and take him on as a hired hand.

He slipped out of the farm that night and hitchhiked the long way back home. Finally, he reached the turn to the road to his father's house. With still a distance to go, he started practicing his apology. With each step, it seemed to come from deeper in his heart. Then he heard a voice call his name. He looked up and saw that his father was running toward him, arms outstretched. They ran to each other and threw their arms around each other in a long embrace, neither wanting to let the other go.

When they finally parted, he began, "Father, please forgive me. I broke our law and betrayed you. I am not worthy to be called your son. Please . . ." He got no further. In his joy, his father called to some servants who had joined in the reunion. He was already giving orders for a party—a joyful celebration involving food, music and dancing to which even the servants were invited.

God kept the younger son safely through his dangerous time of "life in the fast lane," and preserved him in slavery. God's care flourished over this young and foolish man when He helped him come to his senses, recognizing the truth about his father's home. Then He safely brought him the long distance home by foot, restoring him to his father.

We can see two fathers working together in this story— God and the father of the young man. They resemble each other. They're supposed to. The earthly father is supposed to help us understand our heavenly Father.

———◆———

God's loving care in our lives goes back a long way. Like Jim, we have put the past in perspective, recognizing God's care and protection. Like the foolish young man in the famous story, each one of us has come to our senses, returning to God in our own time. On our way back to our true home, we practice our apologies for ignoring His love. He sends His Spirit to meet us when we are still a long way off. God draws each of us close in a spiritual embrace and welcomes us into a new and changed life. All heaven celebrates every homecoming with joy.

Our heavenly Father tells us that He is the God of now. When you and I return God's love, He closes the door to the past behind us and brings us forward into the present. We can live each day in an attitude of joy, drawing on our heavenly Father's strength.

God's Changing Room belongs to us now.

Chapter 5

Change From the Inside Out

When God put His life within our hearts, we began the process of good and godly change. His Spirit touches us on the inside, equipping our spirits with strengths and abilities they did not previously possess.

God calls us to learn a new way of handling things and people. As we put our new spiritual strengths to use, we change from the inside out.

—❈—

Susan learned a new response to a negative situation. It was a silly fight over time off, and it grew from a molehill into a mountain. Claire, Susan's co-worker, was really upset. "You took off early last Friday. Well, that meant I had to stay late because someone had to cover the phones."

"I had the time coming to me, and I only left two hours early."

"Well, you didn't care about my schedule. It was selfish. Just because you're a programmer and I'm only a clerk . . ."

When Susan tried the next day to make peace, Claire delivered the final blow. "I never thought you'd pull rank like that. This has ruined our friendship. Things will never be the same between us again."

"Position has nothing to do with it," Susan tried to say. "It was just an afternoon off."

Claire turned her back while Susan was still talking, and she kept her word. She kept the pot boiling with insults, criticism of Susan's appearance, her work, and her character in general. Every day became such an ordeal that Susan dreaded coming to work in the morning. After a few days, other people came to notice the tension. Susan was a committed follower of God's new life, and she wanted to live in peace and harmony with others. She detested this kind of situation because she thought it put her walk with God in a bad light.

After a few weeks of Claire's repeated digs, Susan stopped caring about peace and appearances. Claire's insults and criticisms made her angry. She wanted to do something about it. This situation was not her fault, and she wanted to let Claire know what she thought, to retaliate in kind. She tried to fight back but always seemed to lose in the war of words. Claire was quicker with the retorts and truly wanted to hurt Susan's feelings. Susan found herself retreating to the ladies' room at least once a day to cry away her frustration and hurt and then compose herself for the rest of the day.

Susan prayed for God to change the situation, remove the problem, or fix Claire. Instead God changed Susan. One night a few weeks into the continuing strife, Susan read the story of Jesus' trial before the Roman governor, Pontius Pilate. Matthew 27:11 said that when Jesus was accused by the chief priests and officials of the temple, "He answered nothing." The governor questioned Him to make sure He understood the many charges they brought against Him. Jesus maintained His silence so that "the governor marveled greatly." Susan heard the still, small voice of the Lord clearly: "That's what I want you to do in this situation. Be quiet as Jesus was. Be silent before your accuser, and you will have power in the silence."

The next day at work, Susan obeyed the still, small voice of the Lord. She wanted to fight back and sling verbal barbs at her accuser, but Susan developed a composed attitude in the face of the challenge to her spirit. It wasn't easy, and it wasn't enjoyable, but Susan put on a patient and quiet spirit and responded with silence to Claire's insults. A few days later, Susan was walking down the hall, biting her tongue after one particularly nasty insult, when God's lightning bolt hit her. *She can't touch the part of you that's most important,* she heard in her heart. *She can't touch Me on the inside, and she can't steal your joy.*

The light came on in Susan's heart and flooded her mind. God was the Sun that lit her life! Joy filled her spirit. Nothing was more important than God's presence with her and in her. The barbs and insults continued several times a day, but from that moment on, they rolled off Susan's back. They produced instead a growing compassion for Claire. Susan thought it seemed sad that she would not let such a silly thing go. Susan prayed for Claire. She asked God to touch her heart and release her from the thing that held her captive.

The barbs gradually decreased over the next month and eventually stopped. One day several weeks into Susan's "silent treatment," Claire asked Susan to join her for lunch. It was the first step in restoring their friendship. Susan rejoiced the day that Claire told her she respected her for the way she had handled the situation.

God gave Susan a chance to put her spiritual strength into practice. She put on the attitude of patience, seeing her adversary, not with anger, but with compassion. Susan put on a mature and quiet spirit, and she grew in inner power. God used her gentle behavior to touch Claire's heart where words and force failed.

——◆——

God changes us through trials and tests. He knows that His sons and daughters grow the most during the hard times rather than the easy ones. We need to keep God in the center of our lives even when going through the trial of a negative situation. We are more aware of God's presence as we follow Him through the test. Our ears hear His voice with a new clarity as He leads us to the trial's successful conclusion. As you and I walk through the trials of our lives toward good and godly change, we learn to respond from an inner position of strength and freedom.

Throughout the centuries, God has worked this way in His people's lives. Many of history's great men and women of God have achieved success in the face of tremendous odds. One example stands out.

——◆——

Paul began his life by establishing his own right relationship with God. Paul (or Saul, his Hebrew name) had it all, even by today's standards. He had a good job, a stellar education, affluence, social position and political influence. Trained by the best Hebrew scholars and an expert in the Jewish scriptures, he possessed a religious fervor second to none. He had all the credentials required by the Law. In his own eyes, he was a righteous man.

Paul persecuted the early church because the new faith appeared to run contrary to everything that he knew to be the basis of a right relationship with God. He believed he was protecting the faith of his fathers when he was present at the death of the first martyr, Stephen. Paul saw this man die a victorious death, but afterward he increased his persecution of the early church. He entered people's homes and hauled men and women off to prison for believing in this "Messiah." Those in Jerusalem who followed the new faith soon came to fear the name of Saul of Tarsus. Armed with arrest warrants, Paul traveled to the nearby city of Damascus to spread the persecution.

God intervened just before Paul reached Damascus. A sudden light outshone the noonday sun, knocked Paul to the ground, and blinded him. Paul heard a voice calling his name and asking, "Why are you persecuting Me?" The voice told him it was Jesus speaking, and that Paul could no longer fight against God's will for his life. Blinded and helpless, Paul submitted to the voice and was led into the city of Damascus. He went without food and sight for three days. Then God sent a prophet to pray for Paul, who then received his sight.

Enlightened as to the true meaning of the new faith, Paul immediately went out and preached as boldly for it as he had once fought against it. He now became the object of an assassination plot, as the persecutor became the persecuted. The followers of the new faith had let Paul down in a basket outside the city wall to save his life. He went next to Jerusalem, preached boldly there, and soon had to flee that city too.

That was just the beginning of Paul's troubles. He suffered hardship, beatings, deprivation, starvation, and shipwrecks. He was persecuted mercilessly by his own countrymen, who now viewed him as a traitor and a heretic. He suffered the loss of almost everything that once mattered to him. He lost his affluence, social standing, religious prestige and even his physical freedom. As the persecution caught up to Paul, he lived the last years of his life in the confines of a prison cell.

Before his imprisonment, he traveled extensively and planted churches all over the known world. Paul followed every trial through to God's successful conclusion. He reached his full potential of godly growth, becoming one of the greatest men of God who ever lived. He touched countless others with the power God gave him.

From his prison cell, Paul wrote letters to the churches he had founded. One written to the church at Philippi shortly before his death is full of joy and peace. Paul's inner freedom triumphed over his physical confinement. The Roman prison could not keep his joy or his maturity from touching others with God's power. The letters that he wrote in A.D. 60 inspire us to this day and lead us in our own lives of good and godly change.

———

God changed Susan through the trial He allowed to come her way. She grew in power as she changed her response to the circumstance. God gave Paul power to touch the lives of others because his inner contentment helped him rise above the circumstances.

Paul's secret of maturity is available to every one of God's people today. The situation we are facing no longer controls us. We control our response to the situation. A newly developed attitude of patience and compassion helps us face the challenge.

God's Changing Room gives us a new understanding of God's ways. Negative situations and people challenge our spirits. Tough situations are where we stretch toward a new level of maturity. This is where we prove how much we've changed and matured. Our tough situation is the doorway to spiritual growth. It changes us from the inside out.

Chapter 6

God Helps Those Who Trust

God behaves like any loving Father. He encourages an attitude of trust in His sons and daughters as they walk in the path of good and godly change. As this attitude of trust grows in our hearts, we turn more and more of our concerns over to Him. Yet there may still be places where unbelief stubbornly persists. God sees ahead in the walk of faith and knows that these areas can hold us back from growing and making needed changes. God works to capture every area of your heart and mine, removing fear and doubt and bringing trust and belief.

Harry needed to receive God's goodness, but first he had to change his attitude to one of belief.

Harry drummed his fingers on the desk and looked at the clock for the third time in the last five minutes. He wanted to know how everything went this morning. Carol, his wife, had taken their three-year-old son to his first day of school. He dialed home.

"How did Michael do this morning?" he asked.

"It went okay," Carol said. "Although it was his first day,

he seemed to take to the new teacher and the aide right away. The aide worked with him one-on-one for a while, and then he started to work with the speech therapist. Everything went well, and I left so he could get used to being there on his own."

Carol and Harry discussed their hopes that the school could make real strides with Michael's speech problems and learning disability. The school was set up to handle special needs like his, and the staff was used to hyperactive behavior, which could be a real problem in a regular nursery school.

After he hung up, Harry tried to get into the paperwork on his desk. He finally gave up, got a cup of coffee, and leaned back in his chair. *Why?* he asked himself. *Why did it have to come to such a painful step as this?*

Michael's developmental problems began in infancy with sleep problems that grew into behavioral problems during the terrible twos. By the time Michael was three-and-a-half years old, he was still struggling with his behavior and having extreme difficulty learning to speak. For most of this time, Harry convinced himself that Michael was just an all-around boy and that he would outgrow these things. He dismissed Carol's concerns about Michael's development as a mother's over-anxiousness for her only child. They enrolled Michael in a regular nursery school, which unfortunately, rather than solving the problem, only drew attention to Michael's inability to socialize with his peers.

In every other way, Michael appeared fine, just like any other child, attractive and cute, and Harry refused to admit that anything could be wrong with the son he loved so much. One Saturday afternoon, however, the painful truth stared him in the face. Carol was out shopping, and Michael stood in front of the refrigerator, trying to ask Harry for something, but Harry could not understand Michael's words. Harry felt helpless as Michael finally began to cry. His small fists pounded Harry's leg in frustration. At that moment, Carol returned and correctly interpreted that Michael wanted a drink of juice. Harry took his son in his arms as Michael's sobs quieted down. Harry's heart broke. What came so easily for other children was so hard for Michael.

After that Saturday, Carol and Harry began to seek help for Michael. A neighbor had recommended a preschool for handicapped children months ago, but Harry and Carol had resisted enrolling Michael in a program that labeled him in such a painfully negative way. The pediatrician referred Michael to a neurologist who diagnosed learning disabilities and prescribed medication for his hyperactivity. This medication led to more medication to counteract the side effects of the first drug.

Anger rose in Harry in the wake of his initial hurt. Why didn't God help them? Didn't He love Michael? Harry came to faith in God's Son during Michael's second year, but in the last few months, Harry's faith seemed to gasp and stutter at the obstacle it was facing. Now he felt only anger toward God and a lack of trust in His goodness.

Meanwhile, Carol and Harry were going in circles, getting nowhere, and Michael was losing pieces of his childhood to a brain and nervous system that would not work together so that he could learn and develop normally. They needed an alternative to Michael's medications and finally decided to enroll him in the preschool, putting his needs ahead of their own pride and concerns.

That night, the night of Michael's first day in school, Harry arrived home to a mini-celebration. Carol made his favorite dinner, London broil with apple pie for dessert, and best of all, Michael met him at the door with the drawing he had completed in school. It was supposed to be a truck, and although it looked more like an explosion of red and yellow crayons, he was proud of it. Michael said he liked his teacher and his new school. Carol added that the teachers confirmed his good day, and the speech therapist thought Michael would make good and steady progress in their program.

Michael did progress that first year in the school. About a month after his enrollment, the director of the school recommended another neurologist, and she proved to be an answer to prayer. This new doctor gradually took Michael off all medications and started him on a special diet that improved his behavior dramatically. With his behavior under better control, Michael could pay attention and absorb more information. The other children also reacted more positively toward him.

On a spring Saturday a year later, Harry was barbecuing on their patio in the back yard. Michael rode up on his tricycle. He said simply and clearly, "Dad, I want some juice, please." When he finished, he "peeled out" around the corner of the patio and back to the driveway.

Yes, Harry thought. *God is good. He must love Michael even more than we do.* While Harry reacted in anger and unbelief, God was already offering solutions.

God gently nudges each of us forward in the life of good and godly change. When one of His children stumbles and falls due to pride or stubbornness, He reaches out a hand to lift that child back to his feet. He is there to guide His sons and daughters into His path of trust and obedience. He knows that these things do not come naturally to any of us, but a heart that is right toward God will soon turn in the direction of His love.

God never causes the situations over which we struggle, but He always has the answers. He turns each of us carefully in the direction of belief, gently influencing us to place our need in His hands through prayer and a continuing attitude of trust. God brings about a deep-seated change in the heart and provides an answer to the need at the same time.

———

In A.D. 30, another father needed God's help for his son. There was no mass media, but the news spread like wildfire. Everyone heard the news quickly. A local carpenter had turned water into wine at a wedding with everyone present. There were rumors of healings and powerful teaching that confounded the scribes and leaders of the synagogue.

One particular man was intensely interested. For him, it was a matter of life and death. He was a wealthy and influential man who had a problem that all his money and influence was unable to solve. His young son was sick. It had begun as a fever and continued unabated until the boy grew weak and thin, his limbs unable to support his weight. The best physicians failed to cure him, and now the father watched helplessly as the boy hovered between life and death. As he looked at the pale face, the shallow labored breathing, the thin body that had only recently been so active in play, he made a decision. He would seek out this carpenter and plead with Him to come and heal his son. He would entrust this mission to no one, but he would carry it out himself.

He left almost immediately and walked all that day and into the next until he reached the town where the carpenter was staying. He found Him speaking to a small group of people in a courtyard. His clothes looked plain and rough compared to the father's rich garments, but there was a presence about Him that made the father approach Him respectfully.

As the carpenter turned to look at him, the father put his urgent plea into words: "My son lies sick at home at the point of death. Please come to my home and heal him before it is too late!"

At his heartfelt plea, Jesus rose and went with him. He may even have put a hand on the father's shoulder to encourage him as He asked the details of the boy's illness. Jesus' closest followers traveled with them, lagging behind as Jesus and the father hurried ahead. Perhaps as they walked together, Jesus explained that His heavenly Father had sent Him to tell people that God is a Father, too. Jesus said the heavenly Father's love is even greater than love from human parents. Jesus said that God wanted to heal the father's son. He explained that miracles and acts of healing were for an encouragement, but that the wealthy man could believe on his own.

Perhaps at that point, the man stopped in his hurried pace and turned toward Jesus. "You mean, I could believe right now, and my son could be healed right away? We don't have to wait until tomorrow when we get there?"

Jesus answered, "Go your way and return home. Your son lives. He is healed."

The man believed Jesus' words and said simply, "Thank You." He turned and started home by himself. With each step, the joy in his heart grew. He trusted the carpenter's words. His son would recover completely. He believed that even now, the color was coming back to his face and strength returning to his limbs. Soon he would run and play, like any other healthy boy.

All that day and into the next, the man journeyed toward home, eagerly anticipating seeing his son alive and well. What a change from his desperate journey two days ago!

Well into the second day's travel, he looked up and saw two men hurrying along the road. As they neared him, he recognized two of his most trusted servants. As he waved, they broke into a run. They reached him, breathless, and burst out together with the good news: "Your son is alive! The fever broke, and he is well!"

The man's heart leapt for joy. "When?" he asked. "When did he begin to get well?"

"Yesterday," they both answered. "Yesterday at one o'clock in the afternoon."

He knew it! That was the exact time the carpenter spoke the words, "Your son lives."

As he hurried the rest of the way home, the father thought about the carpenter. He was no ordinary man. An ordinary man would have come with him and healed the boy. Instead, this man took the time to touch his father's heart and give him a new belief in God's goodness, a belief he could share with his whole household. He approached his house and entered the door. He heard a young voice shout, "Father! Father, I'm well!" And a young boy bounded across the courtyard and into his arms.

God encourages an attitude of trust in every one of His children. Just as Jesus walked with the wealthy father until his heart opened completely in trust, so will He walk with you and me. As God's tender touch softened the hard places of unbelief in Harry's heart, so will His touch soften your heart and mine.

God's fatherly nature prevents Him from forcing Himself on us in any way. God chooses to limit Himself by the boundaries we set with our free will. God gently works to engage the will so that our growth will be healthy, and the changes we make will be lasting and deep-seated.

In *God's Changing Room*, a Father's tender, loving influence brings us to an acceptance of His goodness. He patiently knocks on any door we close off to Him. He waits until we open that door in a growing attitude of trust.

One step of belief at a time, we allow God's help into a new area of our lives. You and I make good changes, changes that bring lasting solutions to our problems. God brings help to those who trust.

Chapter 7

The Mind-Heart Connection

God opens each of our hearts with a desire for the truth and encourages us to gather information about Him. God knows the inevitable conclusion of a search begun with an open mind and heart: We will receive life-changing knowledge.

It is so important that each person begin the search after God. He provides avenues and opportunities to gather information. He wants each person to find out the truth for themselves, to stand on his or her own two feet in faith.

God encouraged Ture to seek after Him with the mind and with the heart. He invited Ture into a search through roundabout means. The year was 1941.

Ture saw her the first time from across the street. She walked into the same branch of the bank in which he worked. He knew right then and there that she was the girl he was going to marry. He learned that her name was Marion, and he courted her over the next two months. Their courtship might have gone on much longer if the war hadn't intervened, but Ture joined the Navy after Pearl Harbor. They wanted to get married before he left to go overseas.

Marion's pastor put up a roadblock. Ture was an atheist, and the pastor said Ture had to be baptized before he would marry them in the church. In 1942, those things mattered more than they do today, so Ture went off to boot camp as a single man. He confided his problem to the Navy chaplain, who instructed Ture in a four-week course in Bible study. During the course, Ture gained mental knowledge about God, and he was baptized in the Navy chapel. He didn't feel any different—he was still an atheist at heart. *Nothing has changed,* he thought, *except that I now hold a baptismal certificate in my hand, and now Marion and I can get married.*

On April 25, 1943, Marion and Ture were married, just before Ture was shipped overseas. Combat experience in the South Pacific made the information from his Bible course real to him. He learned how quickly a man could leave his atheism behind when under fire. Everyone prays in a foxhole, and Ture put his new knowledge to work in prayer. *At least,* he thought, *now I know who I'm praying to.*

After the war, Ture went back to his job in the bank, and he and Marion started a family. The faith experience he had gained in the war faded in civilian life, and he figured that in a real pinch, he could get to heaven on Marion's coattails. Every Sunday, Marion went to church and took the girls to Sunday school. Ture dropped them off, went back after church to pick them up and drove them home.

Years passed, the girls grew up, and Ture continued to stay away from both the church and God. Marion's pastor used another roundabout method. He eventually succeeded in drawing Ture into a private Bible study through their mutual love of history. Ture gained more mental knowledge and came to believe that the Bible was a reliable historical document. He started coming to church and eventually got involved socially, even serving on the church board, feeling comfortable in a setting that reminded him of his job in the bank.

During this time, Ture's mind absorbed more knowledge while God prepared his heart for a new experience. In the mid-1970s, a move took Ture and Marion to a new church in another county. Ture's new pastor planned to attend an evangelism seminar and asked for a volunteer from the church to come with him. At first, Ture resisted the inner urge to speak up, but when no one else volunteered, he felt sorry for the pastor and so he offered to go.

The seminar lasted two days and was held in a motel 200 miles from home. At the end of the first day, Ture went to bed determined to leave first thing the next morning before the next session started. There was no—definitely no way—he was going to do what the seminar was training him to do. He was not going to knock on people's doors, enter their homes, and talk about Jesus.

But God knew better. He knew that Ture needed additional information before he could make an informed decision. The door to Ture's motel room just happened to be broken. He could bolt it but not shut it completely. His room also just happened to be right across the hall from some people who were having a loud, all-night party. The music and loud voices from across the hall, as well as the clanging of the partly open door, woke Ture several times during the night. Each time he woke up, he found himself reviewing the seminar materials and reading some chapters in the Bible. That night, Ture learned that he could not get to heaven on Marion's coattails. He learned that nothing he did for the church on the board or even at this seminar could get him into heaven. Ture knew he was going to heaven, not on his merits or on Marion's merits, but on his own faith. He was going to heaven on Jesus' merits. Jesus' death and resurrection made the way possible for Ture to have new life. This new knowledge changed Ture's mind, changed his heart, and changed his choice.

Ture got up the next morning ready to tell others about Jesus. He finished the seminar, returned to the church, and lead an evangelism team for the next 22 years. He found his niche, not in the church board meetings, but in going out and inviting people to meet the Savior he learned so much about. He kept his newfound enthusiasm because he knew the truth in his heart, and the truth changed him.

Ture served God faithfully until his death in 2001. He ended his life of service to God with Marion at his side. The peaceful presence of God was so strong in his room that it seemed angels waited around his bedside to usher him into his real home. As Ture took his last breath in this life, he passed through death's door straight into the presence of his Savior. He went to heaven, not on Marion's coattails, but on his own personal knowledge of his Lord and Savior.

———◆·◆———

God encourages us to seek after Him with the mind and with the heart. He gives us two basic kinds of knowledge. One builds the mind. It gives mental understanding and basic information about who God is. It teaches that God is able to keep us and lead us in the new life. The second kind of knowledge builds assurance in the heart. It leads to a fuller understanding of God's work in the individual life. Heart knowledge teaches us that God is not only able, but also willing, to help us in the life of good and godly change. Both kinds of knowledge work to our advantage.

God leads us step by step through this learning process. Even one of the original disciples needed time and experience to absorb sufficient knowledge to make the mind-heart connection.

——➤◆◅——

Peter left the boat anchored near the shore and went with Andrew, his brother, to wash their fishing nets. A hard night of fishing with no catch left him tired and discouraged. Peter grumbled and complained to Andrew. Andrew reminded him of the new Teacher they had recently met. He seemed to have the answers they sought, but Peter still couldn't bring in the catch they needed to pay the heavy Roman taxes and buy food for their households. Peter and Andrew dismissed the new Teacher from their minds and fell silent on the way back to their boat.

When they got to the boat, they found the Teacher standing in it and preaching to the crowd pressing in on Him from the shore. He asked Peter to push out a little from the shore and continued to speak to the people. Peter could hardly refuse in front of the crowd. Peter and Andrew and their partners, James and John, became a captive audience to the teaching. As Peter listened, he felt the burden on his mind grow lighter.

The Teacher finished speaking and told Peter to launch the boats into the deep part of the lake and let down the nets. Peter gave Him a professional fisherman's opinion of such a waste of time and effort, but in the end, he said, "Nevertheless, at Thy word I will let down the nets."

Peter, Andrew, James and John took both boats out. When Peter and Andrew let down the net, the fish that hadn't been there a few hours earlier came out of nowhere, filling the net until it broke. Peter and Andrew signaled their partners, who came and helped them. The catch of fish filled both boats "so that they began to sink."

This experience brought knowledge that changed Peter's heart. He fell to his knees and begged the Teacher to leave him and go on to someone else. But the Teacher stayed and encouraged all four of them. He said that He would teach them all they needed to know to reach others with the knowledge of new life.

Peter walked and talked and lived with the Source of all wisdom and knowledge for three years. He saw God's power in action for individuals and for multitudes. He heard the truth from God Himself in human form. Peter heard and experienced it all.

When the Teacher was arrested and brought to trial on trumped-up charges, Peter's courage failed him. His courage failed because his knowledge failed. The information Peter gathered from his senses denied the knowledge in Peter's heart. Peter's world came apart that night. He lacked understanding of the Teacher's predictions of His own death and resurrection. As Peter followed the unruly crowd to the high priest's palace to learn his Teacher's fate, three individual onlookers confronted Peter. Peter denied his association with the Man he had followed so closely. Peter wept bitterly, experiencing deep anguish in his soul.

Peter's next experience with his Teacher restored his heart and gave him the knowledge he needed. On the morning of the resurrection, Peter entered the empty tomb before anyone else. The risen Christ appeared to Peter later that day. Only Peter and his Master know what transpired between them in this private meeting, but this new knowledge and experience changed Peter's life.

The risen Teacher spent several weeks preparing His followers for the coming change in the kingdom of God. His teaching gave them new knowledge and prepared them for a new experience of faith. One morning, God moved powerfully on His followers, and that day the new faith became a church. God filled their open hearts with the knowledge of His presence. Their hearts overflowed with His love. It joined their hearts with their heads in new knowledge born of God's strength. This new godly strength changed the Teacher's followers—and it changed Peter.

As a crowd gathered outside the house where the Teacher's followers had assembled, Peter took charge. A short time before, a mob had cried in these very streets for the Teacher's death, and Peter had backed down when confronted by three individuals. But this morning, Peter boldly stood up before the crowd and shared his new knowledge. Three thousand people joined the new faith that very day.

Peter's strength of conviction stood with him to the end. Tradition tells us he passed the most severe test of martyrdom. He left his earthly life of service to continue his quest for knowledge in an eternity of life and growth. Ture opened the door of knowledge through intellectual study of the Scriptures. Peter entered through the "school of hard knocks." Both Peter and Ture experienced God's strength throughout their lives of service. They lived out their inner convictions in a real and powerful way.

<hr/>

Every day you and I continue our search for more of God's truth. God answers all the tough questions that life forces us to ask. In the reality testing of modern-day life, God fills our hearts and our minds with the truth. He always leads in the life of good and godly change, joining mental understanding with assurance in the heart.

God's Changing Room connects our minds and our hearts. As the heart and mind unite in the same truth, conviction is born in the spirit. Conviction changes and empowers us. It gives us new confidence and assurance. We learn that God's plan for our lives is the most intelligent choice we can make.

We make the mind-heart connection in a lifelong process of learning.

Chapter 8

Nothing Happens by Chance

In the life of godly change, a good and loving God insures the success of each person's walk of faith. Nothing happens by chance. The God who called you and me into His path of life orders our steps and plans every change that comes our way.

Each of us may experience an apparent failure or defeat, but even in this, God is still in control. In every failure lie the seeds of victory. In every defeat, the seeds of success.

Elaine was about to experience an apparent defeat in her walk of faith, but God's power worked on her behalf. He brought good out of a bad change, leading Elaine closer to ultimate victory and success.

Elaine heard the yelling early that night. It was only early evening, and they were fighting again. Elaine, along with Brian and Tricia, her son and daughter-in-law, shared the old farmhouse that had been their family home for over 30 years. This time Brian and Tricia were fighting over finances. They were still newlyweds with a baby who had arrived unexpectedly, and the old house was a constant drain, needing repairs and continual upkeep. Elaine helped them out with the bills and mortgage, but her disability check only went so far.

The baby started crying, and the atmosphere grew so thick with tension that Elaine didn't know what to do. Should she offer to take care of the baby? Brian Jr. was only three months old and probably needed a feeding. But if she asked to help, would Brian and Tricia draw her into their argument or vent their anger on her?

Elaine finally left her room and went downstairs, offering to take Brian Jr. for a while. The baby settled down as Elaine picked him up and changed him. She got out the bottle, warmed it, and had just begun to feed him when Tricia jumped on her. The young mother told her she was spoiling the baby. It was too soon for a feeding. Brian took the baby from Elaine, and she retreated to her room and stayed there the rest of the night.

It was like this almost every night. The weekends were worse. Phone calls were limited in case they woke the baby. Recently, Elaine had had a car accident, and Brian and Tricia had advised her to get rid of the car. Now she felt like a prisoner in her own home. She considered moving in with May, her mother, who was alone now and widowed. Or, her other son, Gary, and his wife were always asking her to come and stay with them. She never accepted these offers because she felt tied to the old farmhouse. It had been the only constant in her life over the last 30 years. She lost her husband several years ago and succumbed to depression, fighting a continuing battle against its shadow and standing firm in faith in God and that His light assured her of ultimate victory.

Elaine also felt obligated to stay and help Brian and Tricia with their finances and the baby. Brian was always telling her that she needed them, that she couldn't handle living on her own. And perhaps, Elaine thought, he was right. She always felt like she was doing something wrong. The tension in the house made her feel unhappy and up-tight.

That night, Elaine tried to pray. She prayed for the fighting to stop. She asked God to bring about a change, to deliver her from the circumstances. The fighting stopped soon after Elaine prayed, and the night remained quiet and calm as the baby settled down to sleep. But Elaine couldn't sleep. Soon she started to cry and couldn't stop. She cried what seemed like an ocean of tears. She cried for herself, for Brian and Tricia, and for Brian Jr. She cried for the whole situation and prayed for a changed life for herself. It seemed so far out of reach.

Two days later, Elaine went to her counselor, and God's deliverance seemed even farther away. The counselor rec-ommended that Elaine be admitted to their inpatient mental health clinic immediately. Elaine was exhausted from a lack of sleep and unable to eat. She started weeping again as she signed the admission papers. This seemed like another de-feat in her battle against depression.

In the hospital, however, Elaine had time to think, pray, and sort things out by talking to her counselor. Freed from the daily tension and fighting, she began to settle into a normal routine. A sympathetic ear helped boost her spirits, but she still saw her hospital admission as a defeat, espe-cially when Brian and Tricia did not come to visit her.

The night before her release, the phone call came that changed everything. At first, it seemed to be yet another de-feat. Brian called to accuse Elaine of leaving them high and dry without a babysitter and ultimately of not carrying her share of the family burden. Then he abruptly hung up. Elaine was so upset that she immediately talked to one of the counselors. As Elaine discussed the call with her counselor, she began to wonder if she should even return to the house. She asked for time alone in her room, where she opened her heart to God. Now that she was removed from the situation, she could see it in a new light. Was God showing her a way out of the darkness that surrounded her? Was He giving her the strength through her hospitalization to make a decision that otherwise would have been too difficult?

A conference that evening between Elaine, May, and Gary resolved the issue of discharge. The hospital agreed Elaine should go to stay with May, her mother, and Gary agreed. Elaine accepted this solution as the Lord's plan and saw a door to a new and brighter future opening up. May was approaching 80, and Elaine could be a help to her in the way of finances and companionship, relieving the stress of May living alone.

Elaine moved on to her new life. God used her hospital stay to bring her out of a bad situation and into a new one. He changed a defeat into a victory. Now Elaine plans for her future, contacts her friends, and has purchased a new car. Best of all, she has a new purpose in making life better and easier for May. The move works well for both of them, giving them the companionship they need. Each day Elaine steps farther into the brightness of God's future, leaving the darkness of depression farther behind.

<hr />

In God's path of life, every change works out for our good. The good changes bring the advantage of new and better things. God's power works through seeming negative changes to eliminate things from our lives and lead us closer to fulfilling His plan for our lives.

The world's process of change, by contrast, is a random process. Some of the world's changes work out to our benefit, and some have a negative result.

God allows nothing to come into our lives that brings lasting defeat. His life within our hearts ensures ultimate success for every failure. You and I come into our next victory, serving God in a bigger and better way than before.

⪢⧫⪡

A story of a young man named John, as told in the New Testament, begins with a failure and builds over time into a success story that still inspires people today. The Bible gives us snapshot views of his emerging victory.

The year was A.D. 47, 14 years after the birth of the new faith, and the location was Perga, a city in southern Asia Minor, on Paul's first journey to spread the new faith to the western territory of the Roman world. Paul and two companions, Barnabas and the young man named John, succeeded in starting churches as they brought the new faith to new areas. But not long into the trip, John suddenly turned back and went home to Jerusalem. Paul and Barnabas finished the journey without him, continuing to start churches and checking up on them on their way back home.

Two years later, we encounter this young man again. He is with Paul and Barnabas at the church in Antioch. Paul and Barnabas prepare to make a second journey to visit the churches they had previously started. John wants to go with them. He apparently has grown and matured, and he wants to overcome his earlier failure. Barnabas wants to take John, but Paul refuses. Barnabas and Paul disagree so strongly over this issue that they ultimately go their separate ways. Barnabas takes John and sails to Cyprus to work with the churches there, while Paul chooses another companion named Silas and sets sail to Asia Minor to visit and encourage the churches. On this trip, Paul finds another young man named Timothy to help him in his work.

That could have been the end of the story for our young man named John, except for the life of God, the power of God at work within. John could have become discouraged and quit. He could have decided that he didn't have what it took, that he couldn't rise above his earlier failure. Instead, John continued to pursue his life of good and godly change. John drew on the strength of his God-centered spirit to rise above his earlier failure. At the moment John decided to press forward, his future success was assured.

The time is now between A.D. 60 and 67. The new faith is over 30 years old. Unfortunately, the persecution of the new faith has spread along with its growth, and those who persecute it now have the backing of the Roman Empire. The followers of the faith are imprisoned, often tortured and executed, and the churches are forced underground. Even the leaders, including Paul, are imprisoned, and some of the original founders of the faith are martyred.

John, our young man who is not so young anymore, proves his courage by visiting Paul in prison and supporting him in the work of the ministry. Paul even sends for him saying, "He is profitable to me for the ministry."

The new faith needs strengthening in its time of persecution. John decides to write a new piece of literature—the first of its kind. It would strengthen the churches under persecution and give them a reliable written record of the events leading up to the founding of their faith. It would comfort all the followers of the faith with an eyewitness account of the life, death, and resurrection of the Savior. It would encourage those who walked in God's light to spread the new faith in spite of the obstacles they faced.

This piece of literature survived and encourages us even today. You know it as "the Gospel according to Mark." Historians tell us that John Mark's gospel was the first of the four gospels to be written. As such, it formed the basis for the gospels of Matthew and Luke, with much of its material repeated in these two later books.

━━◆◆◆━━

John Mark succeeded in his life of good and godly change because his confidence was not in himself, but in the God whose nature dwelled within him. When faced with an apparent failure, he came back stronger than ever by relying on God's power. Elaine needed to make a change in her life, and God used the apparent defeat of her hospitalization to bring her closer to success in life.

For those who walk in life-changing faith, failure or defeat is only a temporary setback. Sometimes God lets us fall so we can learn how to get back up again. It is only after the process is complete that we can look back and see God's good purpose.

In *God's Changing Room*, success comes not from a perfect track record but from picking ourselves up after a fall and getting back in the race. Failures and mistakes become simply things from which we can learn. Through an apparent failure or defeat, God calls each of us forward as we build spiritual muscle for the next success.

Our success in the life of good and godly change depends more on God than it does on us. His Son's sacrifice 2,000 years ago made our new life possible. Now God is on our side, and nothing happens by chance.

61

Chapter 9

Give Up Total Control

God stays on the sidelines of our lives until we come to Him in faith. But as soon as we invite Him into our hearts, He moves from the outside to the very center of our beings.

This is the moment He's been waiting for. Now God can actively participate in our life of good and godly change. His life rises in the heart in a continuous flow. He can speak to us any time, day or night. God walks with us in spiritual partnership.

———◦——◦———

Greg gained a powerful partner when he invited God's Son into his life. He needed God's help to conquer a bad habit.

Greg took his second dose of aspirin after glancing at the thermometer, which read 103.5 degrees. He lay back on the pillows, sipping on the ginger ale his mother brought him. As he dozed off, he realized he hadn't smoked a cigarette in three days—not since he had gotten this cold that turned into the flu with a very high fever. *Maybe something good will come out of this,* he thought. *I could actually quit smoking.*

Four years earlier, Greg had succumbed to peer pressure and smoked his first cigarette. Considered a computer nerd by his peers, and despite the fact that he was a church-going Christian, he wanted to prove he was a "regular" guy and not a geek. Looking back, he bitterly regretted that first cigarette and his many other sacrifices for social acceptance.

In the past few weeks, Greg sensed in his spirit that God wanted him to quit smoking, but he had continued to put it off. At the age of 18, Greg had quite a nicotine habit. He had tried once before to quit with disastrous results. The withdrawal symptoms devastated him in the first few days as he ate himself into oblivion. By the end of the first week, the terrible symptoms were so strong that he began smoking "just one cigarette." Then he smoked another and another. Three weeks later, he wound up smoking even more than before he had tried to quit, and as a result, he was now up to two packs a day.

But Greg had something new going for him. It actually started many years ago in the elementary grades of Christian school when he gave his heart to God in an act of faith. Unfortunately, as he entered his teenage years, that experience faded, only to be replaced by an interest in girls, clothes, cars, and a future career. Then one night, everything changed. Three months ago, something happened that brought his priorities back into focus. One rainy night, while on his way home from his part-time job, he tried to brake on wet pavement to avoid a deer, and his car skidded into a tree. Because he had ignored the simple step of fastening his seatbelt, his head went forward into the steering wheel. His parents picked him up in the emergency room and told him how "lucky" he was to walk away from the accident. He needed surgery for a broken nose, but he was back on his feet again two weeks later.

At that time, he saw what was left of his car at the body shop, and the full shock hit him. He couldn't help thinking, *What if I had been seriously injured or worse? What if my life had ended in that accident? Where would I spend eternity?*

And just as important, *How will I spend the rest of my life now?* His faith experience in early childhood came back to him as vividly as if it had taken place yesterday. He saw his life now as a gift and realized that more than just "luck" was involved. His heart almost burst with the urgency of reestablishing his relationship with his Savior. Two days later, he met with the youth pastor at his parents' church and made a commitment to begin his life of faith anew, to follow God's life of good and godly change, no matter what the social cost.

For the last three months, he had been doing just that. During that time, his coursework improved, and he began to concentrate on his future career in computer technology. But he also kept getting the nagging sensation that God wanted him to quit smoking. Greg was so afraid of failing again that he had put off quitting, but now he was sick and unable to smoke.

How well he remembered his earlier failure! This time, however, his faith gave him courage and an edge he didn't have before—God's help. This time Greg prayed: "Lord, I'm scared. I like to smoke, and I've failed before. I don't know if I can make it through the first week of withdrawal."

Greg clearly heard the still, small voice in reply: "Let's take it one day at a time. Let's see how we do."

Greg felt encouraged. He was already through the first

few days—the days that had done him in the last time. Besides, he was not alone in this battle against a physical, mental, and emotional habit. Maybe God and he together could lick this thing.

Greg gained a partner in his process of good and godly change. The next few days of withdrawal symptoms turned out to be easier than he thought. Whenever the urge for a cigarette came over him, he took a deep breath and called on the name of the Lord. The first week passed quickly without any problems, even after he recovered from the flu and went back to his regular routine. He felt as if an inner strength was propelling him through the usual withdrawal symptoms and lifting him over the rough spots during the day as he went to school. The next week, the urges didn't come as frequently, even at night on the job. Again, that extra strength seemed to help him over any rough spots.

The desire to smoke eventually petered out completely during the third week. Greg stopped thinking about resisting the urge to smoke, and in fact, stopped thinking about smoking altogether. He found himself going through his days and nights as if he had never smoked at all. Four years of a bad habit was gone in just three weeks. A year later, Greg looked back and thanked God. His lungs were back to normal, and he enjoyed having extra spending money as the price of cigarettes continued to soar.

This time was so easy compared to his other attempt, and it cost him nothing but the admission that he needed God's help and couldn't do it on his own.

———✦———

God gives us spiritual strength to accomplish a good change. Human strength is limited to using the mind to control and discipline the energies of the emotions and the physical body. Anyone who goes on a diet or starts an exercise program uses his strength of mind and willpower to bring his body and emotions in line for what he believes to be a good change. Change that goes deeper than the physical requires a different kind of strength. Successful and permanent change is ultimately a matter of the spirit. It requires mental control that joins with the spirit in accomplishing a good goal.

God's strength knows no limits and makes vast resources available to the one whose heart is joined to Him in faith. Godly strength picks up where human strength leaves off. Once we ask God for help, our spirit comes into play and leans on God's Spirit, allowing His strength to bring the mind, will, and emotions into line. With God's strength, the spirit leads the mind and the body through the process of change.

The task ahead may be bigger than quitting smoking or changing some other bad habit. Following God's lead brings the impossible into the realm of the possible. Nothing is too hard for God.

———

Joshua faced an impossible task by human standards. Joshua was to cross the Jordan River at flood stage, leading 600,000 men—plus women, children, servants and livestock—into the land of Canaan. He was to lead a military campaign against the people of the land in their walled cities, vanquishing their experienced armies. More difficult yet, at 80 years of age, Joshua had to gain the confidence of the 12 tribes of Israel. These were the same people who had given Moses such a hard time before Joshua's leadership. They often refused to follow the laws God gave them and re-

belled against Moses, one of the greatest leaders Israel had
ever seen.

Before Moses died, God chose Joshua to replace him.
Even so, Joshua's courage might have faltered as he stood on
a hill overlooking the tents of the people camped in the
wilderness. These people were desert nomads, not soldiers.
They ate funny-looking little round wafers called manna.
Most of them had no battle experience; they grew up wandering in the wilderness.

God knew that Joshua needed His help. He understood
the monumental task facing him. He spoke to Joshua and
gave him the ingredients for success in his upcoming 30-
year leadership of Israel.

God promised Joshua that He would be alongside Him,
just as He had been for Moses. He promised him military
success, and most of all, He promised to be with him wherever he went. He gave Joshua the key to success: having
"good courage" and "staying strong" in the book of the law.
Whenever the responsibilities seemed too great, Joshua
needed to look to God and trust Him to do what Joshua
could not. He could have doubts in his head, but his heart
needed to be filled with good courage, courage toward God.
Strength would flow from God to Joshua.

Joshua passed his first test of courage. He gave orders
for the people to make preparations to cross the Jordan in
three days. As all 12 tribes united and followed his orders,
their leaders gave him a vote of confidence. What happened
next proved that God was Joshua's partner, just as He had
been Moses' partner. He would provide Joshua the same
kind of supernatural strength.

As all the people (a million or more) prepared to cross
the Jordan River, the priests bearing the Ark of the

Covenant moved to the front of the company, along with one man from each of the 12 tribes. The Ark symbolized God's strength and presence, and the people all understood that God's supernatural strength would go with them and their new leader.

As the priests carrying the Ark drew close to the river, which was flooding its banks, the miracle happened. As they took their first step into the water and the soles of their feet touched the flooded riverbank, the water stopped in its flow downstream. It piled up in a great wall of water before the people, reminding them of God's great delivering power when the Red Sea parted as they had left Egypt. All one million plus people passed over on dry ground.

So began a series of victories that led to the Israelites' settling in the Promised Land. In their first battle, they watched the walls of Jericho fall to the ground. After that, they conquered city after city. God led them to change their lifestyle from wandering to settling down, and their occupation from nomads to farmers and merchants. Good courage led Joshua and the people onward through the 30 years of his leadership.

Good courage is humble courage. It admits it needs help. Good courage recognizes that doubt and fear come from an honest recognition of our human limitations. Good courage looks beyond our limits and sees what God can do. It trusts in God's strength and asks Him to add His strength to ours. Good courage means giving up total control and letting God lead us.

Like Greg and Joshua, we no longer battle life's challenges on our own. God leads us through the doorway of change into a new lifestyle of good and godly changes. God knows there are cities to conquer and walls to bring down. He knows exactly what territories are left from the past life of wandering in the wilderness of the world. He understands the task facing you and me. God knows how to touch our hearts with good courage and when to give us His strength.

We cross the threshold into *God's Changing Room*. We give up total control and lean on Him.

Chapter 10

God Brings Promotion

Sooner or later in the life of good and godly change, God chooses each of us for a new task. This new job is a promotion and means that we will be doing new work and handling new responsibilities.

Our initial reaction may be refusal, especially if this is a first promotion. Many candidates decide that God contacted the wrong person and that their qualifications are inadequate for the job at hand. But God's choice is always correct because He chooses a person based on the qualifications of the heart.

It takes courage to lay aside our natural human tendencies and take a step based on the leaning of the heart. God gave Kayla that encouragement through a special friendship. Kayla buzzed the door at the entrance to the nursing home and said hello to the receptionist. She made her way through the lobby and downstairs to join the women from her church choir. They were already grouped around the piano in the lounge, and she took her place among them.

As the group began its monthly volunteer performance

of hymns and "old favorites," Kayla looked out at the audience. About 20 people sat in wheelchairs or on couches, and Kayla's heart went out to them.

Four months earlier, the choir director asked Kayla to fill in for a singer who was unable to attend. Kayla accepted and found herself coming back as a regular. Contact with the residents awakened a nurturing side to her personality she never knew existed. The patients responded well to her, and she felt unexpected warmth as she returned their affection.

As she watched the choir director for the beginning of the next song, Kayla wondered again about her choice of a career. Well into her second year at the community college, she was majoring in accounting and business management. But lately she felt a stirring in her spirit as if God were calling her to something different. The idea of a career in business no longer gave her the sense of satisfaction it once did. *It must be this atmosphere,* she thought, *so many people in so much need.* In fact, she wondered if God might be calling her to be a nurse. She had to admit, she felt a tug at her heart in that direction. *No,* she argued with herself as her head overruled her heart, *I wouldn't be any good at it anyway. I hate the sight of blood. I'm good at numbers and good at organizing things. Accounting is a safe, solid choice for me.* Yet she still felt an unrest in her spirit as the issue kept coming to the surface.

Kayla again looked out over the audience as some of the women joined in, singing "God Bless America." She noticed with a start that Emma Watson, her favorite resident, was absent. In all of her 19 years, Kayla had never met anyone like Emma. Her own grandmother had died when Kayla was two, and Emma was like the grandmother she'd never known. Emma and Kayla developed a strong bond, sharing mutual belief in God. Alone since her family moved out of state, Emma faced her difficult circumstances and illnesses with a courage that was convinced of God's goodness. She occupied her time praying for others and cheering up her fellow residents. Kayla knew her nurse, Veronica, from church, and she, too, enjoyed Emma's smile and sunny disposition.

Kayla often visited in the evenings and discussed everything with Emma—boyfriends, her parents, music, and even her concerns over whether she should become a nurse or go into the world of business. Emma listened and said that Jesus would guide Kayla, and that she should follow her heart in choosing a career and not her head. In response to Kayla's concern over her parents' reaction to her possibly switching career directions, Emma smiled and said to trust the Lord.

The choir performance ended with "Amazing Grace," and Kayla went to find the nurse and learn where Emma was. Veronica said that Mrs. Watson was ill in bed with pneumonia and too weak to get up. She suggested Kayla go visit her. As Kayla hesitated nervously, Veronica encouraged her. "You will cheer her up. Let's go together and have a prayer with her."

Kayla and Veronica went down the hall to Emma's room. As Kayla entered the room, she felt an immediate sense of peace. Emma lay quietly resting, and her eyes fluttered open as soon as the women came in. A big smile spread across her face, and she whispered her hello in a weak voice, and held out a hand. As Kayla took her hand, Emma weakly remarked how glad she was that Kayla had come. She then asked Kayla to read to her from the Bible, which was lying on the table next to the bed.

Kayla softly read Psalm 23. As she finished reading the

words, "Surely goodness and mercy will follow me all the days of my life, and I will dwell in the house of the Lord for ever," she couldn't help the tear that slid down her cheek. Emma patted her hand. "There, there, dear, don't cry. I'm not going anywhere just yet. The Lord still has work for me to do here. And you—you're going to have a wonderful life."

Emma then took Kayla's hand, and her voice became stronger. "Kayla, you have a caring heart. You should use it in your life's work. Let Jesus lead you into His plan for your life. Follow your heart with the courage He gives you." Then she lay back again, tired but still holding Kayla's hand.

Veronica fluffed her pillows to make her more comfortable and suggested they all pray together. As she led them in the Lord's Prayer, Emma started out in a weak whisper and then slipped into a light sleep.

Kayla looked so worried that Veronica took her to the staff break room for privacy. Veronica said that Emma was stronger than she looked and was in the Lord's very capable hands. She paused, then said, "She gave you very good advice, you know. Have you ever thought about being a nurse?"

Kayla's eyes opened wide in shock. "Actually, I sort of have, at least lately, anyway."

Veronica continued, "I've watched you with the residents—all of them, not just Emma. You have a way of making them feel secure and cared for. You would make an excellent nurse. Why don't you give it some serious thought and pray about it?"

On the way home, a sense of peace settled over Kayla's spirit. Maybe her heart was leading her in the right direction, after all. She could check at school about the nurses' training course. "I guess God is calling me to be a nurse. I'll have to talk to Mom and Dad. Maybe they'll continue to help me through school even if I switch majors. If God is leading me in this direction, He will make a way."

The next morning, Kayla's peace mushroomed into joy. Veronica called to say that Emma had improved during the night and was much stronger this morning. It looked like she would soon be back to her old self.

Emma did get well and lived for several more years. She continued her friendship with Kayla all through nurses' training and during Kayla's first job at a local hospital. Kayla's parents did support her, and she felt such satisfaction in her life's work because she knew that God had been the One to call her into nursing. Through the years, she often thought back fondly to Emma and Veronica, who encouraged her to follow her heart down a new and changed path.

———

Through the work of His Spirit, God effortlessly and efficiently manages an organization that spans the globe and extends throughout centuries of time. Like any good CEO, God promotes from within.

God often chooses people whom the world would consider unsuitable for the task at hand. God chooses those who are too young, too old or inexperienced. He chooses the weak from a natural standpoint so that His strength can operate unhindered. In fact, God often prepares us for the task ahead by removing all natural means of its fulfillment. Sometimes when we see our human options fading, we tend to give up. This is the point, however, when God usually steps in and offers us a positive change.

———

God offered Sarah the promotion of motherhood after

she could no longer have children. At the age of 90, and the age of 100 for Abraham, this couple was past the point of enjoying their physical relationship. God had once promised Abraham a son by Sarah, but that had been years ago. Her reproductive cycle had since ceased, and Sarah looked at her aging body and grew discouraged. That was when God finally offered her the desire of her heart.

Even at the age of 90, Sarah still retained some of her youthful beauty. Her looks had been a problem for Abraham in the past. In Egypt, a prince once physically took her away from Abraham, but God protected her and restored her safely to her husband. Then the years slipped by without the promised heir, and Sarah's reproductive cycle ceased. From a human standpoint, it was way too late for them to have a baby.

That was the time God chose to visit Abraham and tell him (while Sarah waited just within earshot) that a year later she would bear him a son. She laughed to herself when she overheard. She looked at her dead womb and her husband's age, and she laughed at the impossibility of the promise.

God heard her laughter and spoke to Abraham, again in Sarah's hearing, saying that nothing was too hard for Him. All they both needed to do was depend on Him and the natural course of life's functions would return to them both. I believe that God made this promise and gave the date of its fulfillment in Sarah's hearing for an obvious reason. She needed to believe as much, if not more, than Abraham. She had to accept God's promotion at this late point in her life, no matter the consequences. Childbirth in 1900 B.C. was a dangerous, uncertain affair. There were no hospitals, no anesthesia, and no C-sections in case of complications.

Sarah depended on God. She had to. She believed He

would restore her reproductive cycle and her ability to nurse. She also believed God would give her length of life to raise her son wisely, instructing him in the things of God. He needed to become capable of managing his father's great wealth.

I believe that as soon as Sarah opened her heart in faith to God, she felt His touch in her body. She had more energy, more stamina, and stood a little straighter. A few days later, she looked in the mirror and saw that her face had fewer lines. Soon her hair returned to its original dark color, and there was a new spring in her step and a sway in her walk. She started to dress more like she used to as her figure regained its youthful suppleness. It probably didn't take Abraham long to notice the change in Sarah. Soon his interest was aroused as he felt new hope and life in his own body grow in response.

Others noticed the change in Sarah's appearance. Her beauty again became a problem. This time a nearby king took Sarah for himself. Again God protected her and brought her back to Abraham.

Shortly after this event, Sarah conceived, carried the baby to term and delivered him safely. She nursed him as her whole reproductive system functioned like new. Abraham and Sarah named their long-awaited, long-promised son Isaac, which means "laughter." Now Sarah laughed out loud and with others for the joy of her new job, that of being the mother of one of the most important men in Jewish history.

Sarah lived another 37 years, dying at the ripe old age of 127. God granted her time to raise her son and teach him God's promises and how to carry on the family name. The Jewish nation was born as Isaac's 12 grandsons fathered the 12 tribes of Israel. But before any of this could come to pass,

Isaac had to believe with the same kind of faith his mother and father had.

Sarah taught Isaac well. He let God lead him in the choice of a wife and bore two sons, Jacob and Esau. Jacob became God's choice for the family lineage. God gave the world the gift of redemption through its Jewish Messiah, who came through the descendants of Abraham, Isaac, and Jacob.

<hr />

God has work for each and every one of us. Kayla's nursing career was individually suited to her. God's power worked through Sarah in a unique way and gave her a place of honor in the Jewish and Christian faiths.

God's Changing Room is a place where ordinary people are equipped to carry out extraordinary tasks. God plans just where and how each person fits into His organizational structure. He has work for each and every one of us.

God chooses ordinary people because He seeks only a willing heart. He seeks someone who will work alongside His Spirit, who will hear His thoughts and plans. God's will brings us a promotion, and it changes us. Then you and I walk in a new spirit of humility.

Chapter 11

Go With God's Flow

God's river of love winds its way throughout our lives, enlivening every aspect of our beings. It fills our hearts to overflowing and then spills out to touch the lives of those around us. Others need to know what we know—that God loves them and reaches out to them with that love.

━━◆━━

Anthony knew firsthand about God's love. Because God loved him, Anthony could get up in the morning feeling good about the day. As he left for work, he laughed to himself. Three years ago, he would have scorned the idea that he would read the Bible and talk to God in prayer every day. Then one dark night, he found himself on his knees, desperately talking to a God he hoped could hear him.

It took a lot to bring a strong, self-reliant man to his knees. His wife of 10 years left him suddenly, and the empty house depressed him more each day. His social life seemed to leave with his wife as he felt increasingly isolated. Financial pressures mounted, threatening the loss of his house. His boss became more demanding at a time when he didn't need additional emotional pressure. He felt adrift, with nothing to show for his 50 years of life. It seemed that no one really cared. But he was about to have a real encounter with the living God. All his years of religious upbringing and tradition could not prepare him for the experience that would change his life.

One night, as it all closed in on Anthony, he plunged into despair that bordered on suicide. He began his prayer that desperate night by protesting to God the unfairness of his life. He blamed God for all that had gone wrong and for the position in which he now found himself. Then suddenly, he clearly heard the still, small voice say within, *You forgot My Son.*

And Anthony had. He treated the teachings of his childhood religion as so much immature nonsense that everyone eventually outgrows. Now he saw an image in his mind's eye. He saw a cross with a man dying on it. He heard the same voice state, *I want you back.* The image changed to a scene of clouds and light breaking through them. The Son of God lived!

Anthony invited Him into his heart. He accepted His saving work on the cross and believed anew in His resurrection. Anthony's conscience came to life, and he asked forgiveness for his past mistakes. He promised God he would do better. He would read His Word every day and spend time in prayer. Just as important, he would change. He would live differently and do the right thing, to the very best of his ability. At that moment, a weight lifted off his shoulders, and he felt the support of an arm stronger than his. The problems were still there, but he was no longer carrying them alone.

Three years later, he had a new credit history and a new boss. A promotion on the job increased his earning potential. He met someone new, and they became engaged.

Inside, he felt hope and a sense of peace. He knew that God cared and his wife-to-be cared. God gave him a new life at age 50, and he wanted to share it with others.

Anthony went on his first sales call. As a sales representative for a moving company, he visited people's homes to prepare estimates for the cost of their move. He knocked on the door, and a woman about 10 years younger than Anthony answered. Her name was Barbara; she was moving, and she needed a quote. As he checked through the house noting the larger pieces of furniture, he noticed a Bible lying open on the dining-room table. When he finished the paperwork, he asked about the Bible. Barbara said, "I was praying for the Lord to send me some encouragement today," and then she started to cry.

She and her husband were in the process of a divorce and had sold their house. Now she was moving to the South to be near her family. She was scared. She had not wanted this divorce, but her husband had found someone new. She and her teenage daughter would have to leave and go far away from the places they knew and loved. And what chance did she have of meeting someone new when she was already in her forties? She felt as if her life was over.

Anthony told Barbara his story, how God had given him a new start in life. Now he was happier than ever and had found the woman God had chosen for him. Most of all, he was different—a changed man. God wanted to do the same thing for her if she would only put her trust in Him. If God could do it for him at age 50, He could certainly do it for her at age 40. Anthony encouraged her to go forward into her new future in faith and trust God to lead the way. He already had a new future mapped out for her.

After they prayed, asking God to bless her move and her new future, Barbara stood up from the table with a new hope in her heart. God had sent Barbara the best encouragement she could ask for. He sent someone who knew how she felt and could show her the way to faith and trust in Him.

God uses time and circumstances to bring us into contact with those in spiritual need. These "chance meetings" have a deeper purpose. God is reaching out to people through us. He wants to speak words of encouragement through you and me. He wants us to point the way to His path and tell others about a better and changed life. Those in need leave these "chance encounters" stronger in spirit and uplifted in mind. God sends us to give others a refreshing drink of encouragement as they travel through the dry spiritual desert of the world.

Early in the first century, a man in need of spiritual drink traveled through the Sinai Desert. He was a powerful Ethiopian leader, second in authority only to the queen in his own country. Far from his home in Africa, he had come to Jerusalem to worship the God of Israel and was now making the long journey back home. His chariot left Jerusalem and headed south through the desert in what is known today as the Gaza Strip. As he traveled along under the shade of his canopied chariot, he turned to the prophet Isaiah and read this scripture:

> *He was led as a sheep to the slaughter; and like a lamb dumb before his shearer, so opened he not his mouth: In his humiliation his judgment was taken away: and who shall declare his generation? For his life is taken from the earth* (Acts 8:32-33).

This One the prophet talked about must be important, the traveler concluded, but he didn't sound like someone in power. Was the man chosen by God? If so, for what? Who was he? The traveler wanted to understand, but he needed help.

Help arrived in the form of one of God's servants, a man named Phillip. Phillip had been in the city of Samaria. The new faith was spreading like wildfire throughout that city, and joy was everywhere as person after person committed their lives to God's care. Miracles were taking place, and lives were being changed. In the midst of the excitement, God's Spirit urged Phillip to leave the city and head south toward the desert on the road to Gaza.

Phillip traveled many miles on foot and finally reached the dry, barren landscape of the desert. He must have walked along rejoicing in mind and heart as he thought of the many people won to the new life in the city he left behind. Then he saw the chariot up ahead and obeyed a new urging of the Spirit to catch up to the chariot and walk alongside. As Phillip did, he heard the man inside the chariot reading aloud a portion of the prophet Isaiah's writing. Phillip must have seen the confused look on the man's face because he asked, "Do you understand what you're reading?"

"How can I," came the reply, "unless someone explains it to me? Is the prophet speaking of himself or another man?"

At this point, Phillip must have realized that this was the reason the Spirit had led him into the desert. The man invited Phillip into his chariot, and as they rode along, Phillip explained that the prophet spoke of another man. He spoke of God's Chosen One, who paid with His life for the sin of all mankind. This Chosen One stripped Himself of the attributes and powers of deity to take upon Himself the form of a human being. He died a criminal's death without uttering a word in His own defense. As He gave up His life on the cross, He said, "It is finished," and ended the reign of sin on the earth. God raised Him from the dead and exalted Him, lifting Him to His side. Phillip explained how God accepted His Son's death on the cross as payment for all sin. Now the river of love can flow in a refreshing current of forgiveness to all who receive God's life.

The man asked Phillip how he could have this new life, and Phillip explained. An act of faith prepares the heart to receive God's new life. The person expresses in words what the heart believes. Phillip also explained that baptism was a second act of faith, showing how the person was immersed in God's healing waters of forgiveness. It was important as an outward show of an inner change.

The chariot drew near a small pond of water, and the traveler asked if he could be baptized. Phillip replied, "If you believe with all your heart, you may."

The man answered, "I believe that Jesus Christ is the Son of God" (Acts 8:37 NKJ).

At that moment, God lifted the traveler out of the world's spiritual desert and set him on the path of new spiritual life. He and Phillip went down into the water, and Phillip baptized him. He must have felt as if his old life was buried in the flow of God's love, for he rose up out of the water rejoicing. His heart overflowing, he got into his chariot singing, and he sang and praised God all the way home. God's love already filled him and soon would flow out to touch his queen and his countrymen.

—◦•◦—

Today God satisfies our need for spiritual drink with His

Chosen One. God's people live in a flowing river of re-freshing healing water. God fills us so full of His love that we enjoy helping others. Like Anthony, we can talk firsthand about God's delivering and saving power. Anthony knew so strongly that God's love was real that his words of comfort brought Barbara new hope. Phillip's willing heart brought him into the flow of God's Spirit and swept him along with its current of kindness. Phillip invited the weary traveler to drink in God's refreshing river of love.

In *God's Changing Room*, love's flow goes deeper within us. It makes us different and sets us apart from the world. Love fills us to overflowing and touches others. It changes them just as it changes us. God's living waters of love be-come a river in which we can swim.

As we go with God's flow, we open the door to spiritual service. We become willing vessels.

Chapter 12

Good Change Begins With Hope

Deep in the human heart lies the need to grow, develop and become the person each of us was meant to be. This need, this hope, calls from within to a higher purpose in life. This voice of hope is the voice of the human spirit.

Often on life's path, however, this need to change and grow becomes frustrated by circumstances beyond human control. Negative changes can lead us down dark and twisted paths. We can find ourselves walking in the opposite direction, away from that hope within.

———————

Stephanie's journey away from God began one day in a hospital room. Pain ripped through Stephanie's heart. Shock, disbelief, and then rage followed in the wake of the pain. Not her mother. It just couldn't be. Her mother was too young to die—only in her 60s—and Stephie had prayed so hard. She turned to God in her mother's illness and fasted, prayed, and sought God that He would not take her mother from her.

In her grief, she ran from the hospital room and stopped in the hallway, leaning against the wall for support. How she needed the comfort of her mother's presence right now, but she was gone. She would never hear her voice again or feel her gentle touch. Stephie vented her grief in a burst of fury against God. She had prayed to Him. It was His fault. How could God take her mother from her? She would never call on Him again, never! From now on, she would handle things her way and make her own decisions.

For eight years, Stephanie kept her word. She turned to drugs to dull the pain of her mother's death. By the time her grief passed, Stephie was hooked. Negative change piled on negative change until Stephie lost her job, her home, and her children to foster care.

One night, Stephanie found herself out on the streets heading to the corner to buy more drugs. Inside her head, a voice cried to her, saying no, but her feet walked toward the corner anyway. She had once thought herself so mentally strong that she would never become like the users she passed on the street, one step from death, their entire lives spent on their habit. Now she looked at them and saw herself. She cried out loud for God to help her stop doing drugs, but no answer came. Tears streamed down her face as she sobbed out loud in frustration and despair.

Stephie reached the corner and bought more drugs than usual. She had made the decision to end her life with an overdose. *There is no tomorrow for me*, she thought, *no hope.*

Meanwhile, the Spirit of God was about to touch Stephie's spirit with His voice of hope. Back in her room, she prepared to take the fatal overdose and end her life. But before she could take the pills, she heard a voice within her say, *You are battling against a spirit. You can only fight a spirit with a stronger Spirit. Only My Spirit is strong enough to help you.* Stunned, Stephanie let the hope rise within her. For the last eight years, she had defied God and blamed Him for her mother's death. Would God help her, even now? She struggled, afraid to hope.

Hope in her spirit won over death. She left the room and the drugs.

Once she surrendered to the hope within, things happened quickly. Outside in the street, the first rays of dawn lit the sky as Stephanie walked across town. Still in despair, but led by the hope within, Stephie broke her usual pattern, took a new street, and came to a different corner. She found herself in front of a halfway house with a sign that said, "Need help? Come in." Drawn inside, she talked to the workers at length. They called a counselor who arranged for her to enter a drug rehab program. He drove her to a detox center to begin the program.

Everything happened so quickly that Stephie felt like she was being carried along by some good and powerful influence. As the counselor let her off at the detox center, he turned to her and said, "God bless you."

Stephie felt a wave of peace wash over her as the three simple words penetrated her spirit, bringing love and comfort in place of grief and pain. In her new room later that morning, Stephie fell to her knees and cried out with her whole heart to God. She asked for and received forgiveness for the last eight years, and then she asked, "Please take away the desire for the drugs. Take it all away. I want to be free, and I can't be free without Your help."

At that moment, God set Stephanie free. The habit, the addiction, the desire left completely, never to return. Something new replaced it. God gave Stephie peace and comfort and joy. She sensed His presence so strongly that He seemed physically real. All through her time at rehab, she looked for Him, half expecting to bump into an angel coming around the next corner.

God's Spirit stirred Stephanie's spirit with hope and she responded. His touch on her spirit made the hope within her real. God gave her new life.

———

God created the human spirit and planted the seeds of hope deep within the heart. Part of our eternal nature, these seeds live forever in spite of circumstances, the world around us and even our own will. Each human spirit wants to connect with God, to align itself with God's purpose in life. And God responds in a loving way to each person's whisper of hope. He magnifies the voice of your spirit and mine, adding the voice of His Spirit to ours.

God calls us back to that inner hope no matter how far down the road of negative changes we travel. Nothing can silence that voice within because its promise is real. God approaches us quietly and in gentleness. He waits until we can hear our spirit's whisper of hope. Then at just the right moment and in just the right way, He acts to get our attention. He invites a positive response.

———

Early in the first century, Jesus touched someone whose heart still stirred with hope. She had traveled far down the road of negative changes. Jesus had very good news for her, and for us, too, for we of our day and age can identify so well with this nameless woman. Perhaps more than any other biblical character, she speaks to our modern time of emptiness, disillusionment, and negative changes that lead to failure and despair.

The gospel of John tells the story. Jesus took a roundabout route from Judea in the south of Israel to Galilee in the north. He went into the region of Samaria and stopped at the town of Sychar. Around noon, Jesus sat alone at the town well. He was hot, tired, dusty, and thirsty from traveling by foot. A lone woman approached the well to draw water. Sychar's well amounted to the town's community center; it was an informal meeting place, especially early in the morning or late in the afternoon. It was unusual, however, for someone to come to the well in the heat of the day.

Jesus began the conversation with this woman as He sat on the edge of this deep and ancient well. He talked with her about living water that satisfied inner thirst. Jesus compared it to a hidden spring of fresh, flowing water welling up within those who responded to God's touch on their spirits. She asked for this flowing source of water, and Jesus told her to go and get her husband. When she admitted that she had no husband, Jesus revealed the truth: She had been married five times and was now living with someone new. The fact that she was living with husband number six leads us to believe that these were, in part, failed relationships and not marriages dissolved due to death.

The woman acknowledged Jesus as a man of God and changed the topic of conversation to religious differences between her people, the Samaritans, and His people, the Jews. Jesus made the conversation personal again, as His reply stirred her spirit with hope.

Jesus explained that God is a Father who loves and cares about His people. God is a Spirit who goes wherever His people are. He wants them to know the truth more than He wants to them to follow rules and traditions. The hope of a new life is real because God Himself is the hope of His people. He reaches out to each and every one of His people with the good gift of a new and changed life.

The woman's spirit came alive with expectation. The only thing that mattered to God was the hope inside her heart. Could this man be the One, the One whom God was to send to show them the way to this new life? She asked Jesus when the Messiah would come. Jesus said, "I that speak to you am He" (John 4:26).

Life-changing faith welled up within her spirit, filled her being and overflowed to those around her. She went straight into Sychar to spread the good news. This woman who had been afraid of the well at the busy parts of the day now went boldly up to everyone she met and told them about Jesus. She became the first, and perhaps the most successful, person in the New Testament to lead people to faith in Jesus. She brought the whole town out to meet Him.

What a scene that must have been as Jesus and His disciples sat around the well. First they heard some voices, and then some more voices, as a group of people approached the well with the woman in the lead. What a change from her earlier lonely approach! Here she was with lots of people (a crowd, really), talking excitedly, trying to be heard over the noise and the dust of their approach. As the disciples tried to see into the glare of the hot noon sun, they could hear her joyfully saying, "He told me everything I ever did . . . yes, all about my life. He must be the One we are waiting for, the promised One. Come, come and meet Him! Hear for yourselves . . ."

The townspeople did hear. Some came to faith because of the woman's words. Some more came to faith through Jesus' own words. Many received God's touch of life in their spirits.

Stephanie received God's touch in her spirit, and He made her hope real. God gave Stephie a new job, provided a new home, and restored her children to her. Nine years later, Stephanie still praises God for the good changes in her life. God gave the Samaritan woman new life and a new calling. Through her, an entire town received God's gift of a new and changed life.

God's love is the reality behind the appearances of everyday life and the distractions of the world. He continues to love us in spite of the road of negative changes we travel. God loves you and me with an unconditional love, the kind of love we find hard to understand. The obstacles that we think are there exist only on our side of the relationship.

Listening to our spirit's whisper of hope opens the heart to God's love. His Spirit touches our spirits, and God makes the hope of a new life a reality. Something new and powerful, strong and capable comes to life within each of our hearts. It changes who we are.

God's new life lifts us off the dark and negative road we are traveling, turns us around and starts us off in a brand-new direction. Hope is our doorway to *God's Changing Room*.

Chapter 13

Develop Spiritual Roots

God plants His seed of life deep within the heart. Spontaneously this seed begins a process of growth that is at once miraculous, and yet something we experience on a daily basis.

Just like a seed in nature, roots develop beneath the ground, and then the plant grows toward the surface. Sometimes the shoots of new life are barely visible as they break through the soil into the sunlight.

God showed Lori that His seed grows in the lives of our loved ones even if they—and we—are unaware of it.

"Hi!" Kristen called and waved across the parking lot. Lori hurried to join Kristen and her baby, Irina, who was now almost two years old. Kristen and Lori used to work together before Kristen left to have Irina. They hugged and reminisced and exclaimed over how big Irina was getting. Kristen lived with both parents and was attending school for her master's degree. She raised her child in her parents' house so that Irina could have the advantage of a safe and stable environment. Irina was beautiful and tall for her age, already following in Kristen's footsteps. Kristen couldn't be happier, she said.

As Lori got back in her car, she felt a lump in her throat. She hadn't seen her younger son, Jason, in several months although they lived in the same area. He had been on his own for three years, having left home soon after her remarriage. Granted, he worked nights, and she worked a regular nine-to-five schedule, but this time it had been almost four months since she had seen him.

Jason held a special place in her heart, and the years of teenage rebellion triggered by his father's leaving home only served to deepen her concern for him. She waited for him to contact her, calling him infrequently for special occasions, not wanting to be a nagging mother. Lately, however, his calls had stopped altogether, and his lack of contact upset and worried her.

Two years ago, he had been in a car accident and had fractured his nose and a facial bone. Then just last year, he had fought with his brother and moved out of the apartment they shared and into a room in a friend's house. This "friend" left a lot to be desired, and Lori often feared for Jason's safety and well-being. She was glad to hear from his brother that a month ago he had moved into a small basement apartment in a family home.

Lori continued to pray for Jason. With a glimpse of spiritual insight, she recently began to pray for God to bring Jason back to a rebirth of his childhood faith in God. She believed that the truth he knew as a child still lived in his heart in seed form. The potential for a life of faith still dwelled within Jason. A return to God's way of life would bring him the positive and long-lasting change that would give him a new start. Lori trusted God's promise to bring her whole household into His plan for new life, a productive life of good and godly change.

Lori had more peace since she started praying this way, but she still had no more contact with Jason than before. *This,* she said to herself, *is where faith comes in. I believe without seeing that God is working in Jason's life.*

Two weeks later, Lori was sitting at her desk at work. Because her back faced the door of her small office, the familiar voice came from behind her. "Mom, oh, Mom." She turned, and there stood Jason. *I will not spoil this by crying,* she said to herself sternly as she jumped up and they hugged in greeting. Jason explained that he had two days off from work and enjoyed being on a "normal" working and sleeping schedule. He needed certain things that had been stored in her basement for his new apartment. She gave him the key to her place, and they talked some more a short time later when he returned the key. Then she had to go back to work. Just before he left, he wrote down his new address and handed it to her. It looked vaguely familiar, but she dismissed it from her mind as she enjoyed the memory of his visit, his sense of humor, and the way they joked back and forth.

A few minutes later, Lori heard another familiar voice outside her office. It was Kristen and the baby. People who used to work with Kristen gathered around to visit and "ooh" and "aah" over Irina, who was beautiful as always.

Lori thanked God that evening for Jason's visit and his well-being. The next morning as she left for work, she felt a twinge of disappointment. It had been so good to see Jason yesterday. This day would have to take second place to yesterday's surprise.

Lori's phone rang around 10 a.m. It was Kristen.

"I have to ask you a question," she said. "What's your son's last name?"

"Garrison," Lori answered, puzzled.

94

"Then," Kristen declared, "he's living in my house!"

"What?"

"He's renting our basement apartment. He just moved in a month ago, and I haven't seen him because he has his own entrance and he works nights. When I came to your office yesterday, I saw him on his way out, and it took me until last night to put it together. My father," she continued, "thinks he's great." And she added, "He's safe here."

Lori rejoiced in her heart. She knew her battles of faith still raged where her younger offspring was concerned. She had to fight concern for his well-being and hurt over his lack of contact. But now she saw a glimpse of God's work in Jason's life. God was developing in Jason a root system that would one day carry the spiritual nourishment of a new and changed life.

<hr/>

God's seed of life often works underground in our lives and in the lives of others who are close to us. Our natural eyesight looks and sees an absence of growth and a lack of results. But spiritual eyes look with faith and see with the vision of trust in God. The most significant changes often develop away from human sight.

In each person's walk of faith, there can be long stretches of time when it seems as if nothing is happening and all development is somehow stalled. Things can even appear to be going backward, and negative changes are the only things that show above the ground. Every now and then, however, God parts the curtain between the natural and the spiritual, teaching us to see with the eyes of faith. He delights us with a new result of the process of growth.

<hr/>

The small band of followers saw no growth at all. That first resurrection morning, they saw only confusion and despair. One thing was clear—the tomb was empty. There was no doubt about that. The men and the women even agreed on that, but everyone disagreed on the rest of the story. The women who went to the tomb claimed they had seen angels who said He had risen from the dead. Some of the men went to the tomb and saw only an empty grave.

Two of the men discussed these events that afternoon as they walked from Jerusalem to a village about seven miles away. They walked through the streets of the city where three days ago the mob had shouted for His death. They passed by the spot outside the city wall where He died on the cross. All of Jerusalem had seen Him die. And now, three days later, His body was missing. He had said more than once that He would die and rise again. Could this be what He meant? They wanted to believe the women's story. But if it were true, why just an empty tomb and no other visible evidence?

Their conversation went in circles as they searched for an answer. They didn't see the stranger until He joined them. He asked them what they were discussing so intently and with so much concern. They exclaimed that He must be new to these parts and launched into a full explanation.

His name was Jesus of Nazareth. They all believed He was the Messiah. He could have united Israel and restored her people, delivering them from all that held them captive. They told of His miracles and powerful teaching. Fear had gripped them when He had been arrested three days ago. He was tried and condemned by the Jewish leaders and Roman governor. When His followers buried His broken and battered body, it seemed as if all hope lay buried with Him beneath the ground.

This morning, the women had gone to the grave and found it empty. They returned with excitement and a message from angels that said He was alive. Some of the men also went to the tomb but saw no sign of Him or of angels.

"Fools," the stranger said to them. "You need to believe the witness of your own hearts and the words of the prophets." He began at the beginning and verse by verse from Old Testament Scripture explained that the Messiah was to come twice. First He would come as a suffering servant to redeem God's people, and then He would come again in glory and power as a king. The stranger walked with them the better part of the seven-mile journey. He taught them as God's Word worked in the ground of their hearts. It developed roots that carried the nourishment of faith to their minds.

When the two men reached their destination, the stranger took His leave of them and kept on going. They had to hear more! They called after Him and followed Him, asking Him to stay with them. He agreed and went with them to their lodging for the night.

Soon the evening meal was ready, and they all sat down to eat. The stranger took the bread, gave thanks, broke it, and gave some to each of them. As each man took the bread, he looked directly into the stranger's eyes, and their eyes were opened. It was Him! Then suddenly He was gone from their sight.

They rose to their feet immediately. "Did you feel the fire of His teaching in your heart?"

"He stirred our hearts with His words and opened our eyes to see Him."

"We have to go back and tell the others."

"Yes, He is alive!"

They left the meal untouched and hurried back to

Jerusalem to tell the others. They arrived in Jerusalem to find all of His followers—men and women—in an uproar of excitement. Jesus had appeared to Peter, the leader of the group! Now they all believed. As the two men told their story, Jesus Himself appeared in their midst and spoke to them, comforting and teaching them all.

———◦•◦———

Today the risen King lives in our midst. Like He did with Jason, He works under the surface of our awareness, developing a root system of faith. He walks along the way with us just as He did with the two men on the first resurrection morning. Our spiritual roots develop as we follow their road from the cross to the empty tomb to His life in our hearts.

God roots the seed of life securely in our hearts. *God's Changing Room* opens the door to spiritual understanding as we walk by faith and not by sight. We grow on a daily basis because God's life stirs our hearts and sets them on fire.

Our new life begins and ends in our risen King.

Chapter 14

Key to Victory

The life of good and godly change is like a road leading off into the distance. God knows the way around each difficulty on that road. He foresees every event and plans the way to overcome every obstacle.

Sometimes the obstacles we encounter on the road of new life come from without—from people, events, or circumstances. Sometimes they come from within—from the old nature wanting to reassert itself and do things "our way." Sometimes both of these forces unite in a real battle for control of the new life.

———✦———

The day Andrea fought her battle began as usual. Her two daughters went off to the community pool before leaving for their part-time summer jobs. Andrea cleaned the house and looked in the paper for ads for a full-time secretary. She paid her mortgage with the last of the money in her account. Then she went out to the mailbox and found the letter from her husband.

He had left several weeks ago after 23 years of marriage and was staying out of state with other family members.

Looking back at the whole situation, she realized now that God had strengthened her ahead of time to bear the unhappy truths about her deteriorating marriage. Months ago, she had taken a first step toward employment, after 15 years of stay-at-home motherhood, and found part-time work as an evening receptionist. The job built confidence in her ability, her appearance, and her personality.

Andrea knew God gave her strength as one ugly truth after another about her marriage came to the surface. Suspicions of an affair were confirmed when she caught her husband in an outright lie. He betrayed her again with his own family. He attacked her verbally about her faith in God. He criticized his own daughters unmercifully. This unhappy, conflict-filled atmosphere was no way to bring up children. When Andrea confronted him with the truth about their marriage, he left without a backward glance.

On her own, Andrea continued to regain her confidence and to exercise her faith in God freely. She reached out to her family, opened her own bank account, and contacted a lawyer. She looked for a full-time job and spent quality time with her daughters. There were rumors at work that the full-time secretary was planning to leave two months later in September, and that Andrea was being considered for the job. But because of the cost of living on her own as a single mother, she needed to find full-time work before then. She believed that with God's help and guidance, she and the girls could make it in their new lives.

Andrea had not heard from her husband in several weeks, and now she was afraid to open his letter. As she read it, Andrea broke down and cried. He had written to say that he was removing all financial support except the bare minimum he had to leave her by law. The bulk of the income he kept for himself and did not intend to contribute toward the support of his daughters. All credit was now in his name, leaving Andrea without a credit history. He knew the mortgage was $900 a month and that she made $125 a week at her part-time job. He knew the electric bill, phone bill, car and insurance notes would be impossible for her to pay.

All the old weaknesses rose from within her heart. Fear over finances threatened to overwhelm her. Emotional hurt over his lack of a desire to support his own children made her angry. She felt helpless. Then the worst enemy of all attacked—self-pity. Just in time, Andrea remembered God. She went upstairs to the bedroom where she kept her Bible, got on her knees by the bedside, and spread the letter open on the quilt. Tears silently falling, she opened her Bible and put it right next to the letter. *God,* she prayed, *I need Your help. Don't let me be afraid. I want to trust You and Your promises. Show me what to do, how to handle this.*

God spoke to Andrea's heart through an Old Testament prophet. Through words almost 3,000 years old, God touched Andrea's spirit. He told her she was not to fear or be overwhelmed by what lay ahead. He told her that He was her God and that she could lean on Him. Her strength came from Him, and He would support and help her through her problems. He would never let her down.

Andrea put down her Bible, and light touched her heart. She saw her situation in a whole new way. This battle was not really about finances or her wounded self-esteem. This was a fight over her new life of good and godly changes. It was an attempt to make her doubt the future God had planned for her.

Andrea decided to take control through her spiritual nature, and something confident and strong rose on the inside. She asked for God's help in her pressing need—finding full-time work as soon as possible. She prayed and felt God's peace and presence near her. It would be okay. Everything would be okay.

Andrea went to work that night calm on the inside, even though there was nothing new on the outside. The full-time secretary again said she was not leaving until September, almost two months away. Andrea thought that God must want her to look somewhere else for a job.

The next morning dawned as a hot, humid July day just like any other-until the phone rang. It was her boss. That morning, the secretary had unexpectedly given her notice, deciding to leave a month earlier than planned. They wanted to bring Andrea in for four weeks of on-the-job training. She could start next week in the full-time position at her new rate of pay. Oh yes, they would discuss her raise to the secretary's level of pay when she came in that afternoon. Andrea put the phone down, went upstairs, and fell on her knees in thanksgiving in the very same spot where she had cried out to the Lord just the day before. She would be able to pay her mortgage next month and the month after that. She and her daughters could move forward in their new changed life.

Andrea gained more than a temporary victory over financial troubles. She opened her heart to all God planned for her. She obtained training and experience that prepared her for the new jobs God brought her way. She gained confidence, preparing her to accept other major life changes. Unknown to her, God planned for Andrea to marry again. She would meet her future husband at this job, and he would be a man who wanted to walk with her in the new life of good and godly changes.

God gave Andrea the key to victory when she turned to Him. He gave her spiritual strength to close her mind to the voice of her old nature. The storm still raged temporarily on the outside, but inside, her heart rested in peace.

———◆◆◆———

Two thousand years ago, God defeated the god of our old nature. The death, resurrection and ascension of God's Son won a decisive victory that delivered you and me from the god of wrong turns and dead-end paths. Now this temporary god can only try to influence us through bad habits, attitudes, and weaknesses. He threatens from a distance, trying to make us retreat and take a step back from the new life of faith.

The new nature, born of a right relationship with God, overcomes the enemy within. In spiritual strength, we turn our faces toward God. Like the spoiled child that it is, the old nature may throw a few temper tantrums for attention, but eventually it will retreat into a corner. Silenced by the peace ruling in our hearts, it sulks while God brings the victory in every battle, no matter how big or small.

———◆◆◆———

The Old Testament tells of many battles won against tremendous odds because God's people turned to Him in faith. No one needed God's military strength more than one king in 850 B.C.

King Jehoshaphat reigned in Judah, Israel's southern kingdom, for 25 years. He made good changes. He stationed soldiers in all the defensible cities, removed all the places where the people had sacrificed to false gods, and sent teachers out to the towns to instruct the ordinary citizen in the practice of God's law. He even appointed trustworthy judges in all posts in the land. Jehoshaphat had every reason to believe peace and prosperity would be the hallmarks of his reign, that good and godly changes would befall his people.

Instead of peace and prosperity, however, he was handed a king-sized problem. Three armies, old enemies of Israel, massed together and marched against the kingdom of Judah. Outnumbered and outmanned, Jehoshaphat feared for himself, his kingdom, and his people. Warfare in 850 B.C. was not a pretty sight. There were no peace treaties, no negotiated settlements, and no plans to avoid civilian targets. This battle, if lost, meant a great slaughter—certain death for the royal family, torture and death for all prisoners, and slavery for all survivors.

Jehoshaphat set his heart toward the Lord. He proclaimed a fast throughout all Judah. All the men, women and children gathered in Jerusalem. They assembled in the court of the Temple as Jehoshaphat led a "mega" prayer service. He stood before the people as their leader and prayed to the God of Israel. Jehoshaphat praised God for His goodness and greatness in the past, and for His promises to respond to His people's cries for help.

In the silence that followed, God spoke through a prophet. He spoke words of encouragement, deliverance, and instruction, words that ring true even today. God told the people not to fear. He told them where they would find the enemy armies and instructed them to march out the next morning to meet the enemy in battle. Then He made an amazing promise:

Ye shall not need to fight in this battle: set yourselves, stand ye still, and see the salvation of the LORD with you, O Judah and Jerusalem (2 Chron. 20:17).

The king bowed and lowered his head. The people responded in one accord. Hundreds, perhaps thousands, of people in the courtyard of Solomon's beautiful and impressive temple knelt before God's presence. Then the choir of priests raised their voices in a hymn of praise to God.

The next morning, the unity continued. The people and the king marched out to the enemy's position. They began the ascent to the pass at the top of a cliff in an unusual way. To climb to high ground made good military sense. The next part did not make sense, but then Israel's military history was full of victories from battle plans that made no sense. The king gave the order, and the choir set out ahead of the army. Jehoshaphat encouraged the people to trust God, not just for a victory, but for continued prosperity.

The choir went first and started to sing and praise God as they climbed to the top of the cliff in their priestly robes. As soon as the choir started praising God, the victory happened. God fought the battle for them as the army marched behind the choir. They all climbed up to the pass and took their position on the high ground. In the meantime, two of the enemy armies turned against the third and destroyed it. Then these two armies turned on each other, slaughtering themselves. When Judah's army reached the top of the pass, an amazing sight met their eyes. Down beneath lay the dead bodies of all of their enemies.

It was just as God had spoken through the prophet. Not one of the king's soldiers had to so much as lift a sword. Jehoshaphat "set his heart to seek the Lord," the soldiers stood in God's battle position in faith, and they all saw God's victory. Each soldier returned home with increased riches from the spoils of war. None of the other neighboring kingdoms wanted to test their armies against Judah's God, and so the kingdom had peace for many years.

God puts the key to victory in our hands. As God's people, we stand opposed to the negative path of the old nature. We climb to the high ground of the Spirit and turn our backs on the self-defeating cries of the enemy within. Standing in spiritual strength opens the way for God to bring the victory in the outside circumstances of life.

Andrea believed more in God's good future than in the enemy's bad one, and her heart opened to all God planned for her. Jehoshaphat turned his face toward God and won a major victory for his people. A whole kingdom entered a time of peace and prosperity.

God's Changing Room is a place of forward progress, but it also has an expansive quality. As we get better, the changes get better. Good and godly changes come faster, affecting more of our lives.

The key to victory unlocks the door to spiritual success. You and I go forward with a heart open to all God has for us.

Chapter 15

Take God at His Word

As we move forward in our continuing process of change, there are times when we need to leave certain things and situations behind. God wants to bring us a new change to keep pace with our developing spirits. God prepares us for future change by asking us to trust in the promises in His written Word. Should a problem or obstacle appear, God still asks us to take Him at His Word.

Brigette was doing fine in the life of good and godly change. As she walked with God, He provided her with a home. For more than two years, she was very comfortable. Then Brigette came up against a problem stuck right in her path.

The day Brigette moved in, she had hung the drawing by the entrance of her new apartment. The beautiful old house in the picture rested on an Old Testament Bible verse: "My people shall dwell in a peaceable habitation, and in sure dwellings, and in quiet resting places" (Isaiah 32:18). As she stepped back to admire it, she thought the house in the picture looked somewhat like her new home. She felt God's presence there. With His help, she would be strong and at peace in this new place.

Brigette settled in, and two-and-a-half years went by quickly. Then her neighbors moved out of the downstairs apartment. A month later, the landlord told her he had rented it to new tenants. One Saturday she got a look at her new neighbors, and an alarm sounded in her spirit. Four young people—three men and one woman, all in their twenties—moved in downstairs with two guitars, several amps, and very loud speakers.

The electric guitar woke her with a start a few nights later. She jumped straight out of bed. *That speaker must be right under my bedroom!* she thought as she looked at the clock. Two a.m.! The next two noisy hours were a nightmare. By the time she had enough energy to get out of bed the next morning, she was late to work. She tried complaining to her landlord and talking to her neighbors, but it only added fuel to the fire.

Two weeks later, Brigette's neighbors hit their stride. It was party, party, party, with no consideration at all for her need for sleep. She left for work just before 8 a.m. after another impossible night, treating her now-sleeping neighbors to a few slammed doors. On the way out, the drawing and the Bible verse caught her eye. She peered at it through puffy, sleepless eyelids. Where was her peaceable habitation and quiet resting place? She liked it here—or she had at one time. She didn't want to think about the hassle of finding another place and moving. She slammed the outside door even harder on the way out.

The verse stayed with her all day. It promised one thing, but her circumstances shouted another. That evening she opened her Bible to these words:

The Lord is my shepherd . . . He maketh me to lie down in green pastures: He leadeth me beside the still waters (Psalm 23:1-2).

This "pasture" had once been green and the "waters" still. Brigette found another verse about a house. It talked about building a solid foundation by listening to God and doing what He said. Could God be telling her something she didn't want to hear? Was He leading her to a new place?

Brigette went to sleep that night (thankfully a quiet one) thinking about the kind of place she had always wanted. The house (it would be a house) might be small, but she wanted it all to herself, and she wanted it secluded for privacy and quiet. She wanted to have her friends over. A fireplace would be nice for effect and for help with heating. She whispered, *And a garden, Lord. I've always wanted to grow my own vegetables and flowers.*

Over the next few weeks, the possibility of her new home became an inner conviction. She thought about the house founded on the spiritual rock of inner strength, and she thought about the Good Shepherd leading her to another greener pasture. She had to leave, and God had a new place for her. The battle still raged noisily around her, but her belief in God's provision and care for her won out. The Bible verse about God's people dwelling in a peaceable habitation, sure dwellings, and quiet resting places was true, and God would change the circumstances to fit the picture.

Brigette took boxes home from work and started packing even before she found a new place. She let her lease run out. February was the last month of her lease, and as it approached, Brigette was strong in spirit. It was a good thing, too, because she was tried in every other way. The party lifestyle of her neighbors still gave her sleepless nights, and the insecurity in her own home wore her down emotionally.

On a cold Saturday morning in February, Brigette experienced God's personal touch. She sat in her car just outside the Laundromat, but she could not decide which direction to take in her search for a new home. She asked God for an answer. After a while, she said, "Okay, Lord, I'll turn right." She turned right out of the Laundromat parking lot and there it was, two houses on the left! The house had a new "For Rent" sign in the yard. It was on a wooded lot, small, and set back from the street.

Later that day, when Brigette looked at the inside of the house, she felt her excitement mount—a living room, bedroom, and kitchen—all set on two acres. When she saw the wood stove and large vegetable garden, she could have cried. The only problem was, the price was out of her range. What happened next had God's signature all over it. The owners came down $200 in rent and waived the security deposit. Brigette told them that "God led me here, and I think this is meant to be." They replied, "We feel like God brought you to us, and we want you to live here." They chose Brigette over all their other callers and never even put an ad in the paper.

Brigette moved into her new home and felt God's presence immediately as she and a friend dug and planted her spring garden. She knew His touch as she relaxed in front of the wood stove on cool spring nights.

———❖———

When we hold God's Word in our hearts, we come through problems in better shape than before the problem started. His promises give us inner strength. Then the fulfill-ment of His promise brings another good change into our lives. God's Word brings the double benefit of life to our spirits and good change to our lives.

God's promises in His written Word always work. They remain true throughout the changing times of this uncertain world. The word God keeps for us today is the same word He's been keeping for centuries.

⟫═•═⟪

During a first-century synagogue service, God powerfully touched a woman. The same promises you and I believe today set her free so long ago.

The worst kind of negative change came on her sud-denly when she was young and beautiful. It happened the day the Roman soldiers came and took a neighbor off to prison. The screams from the nearby house frightened her as the soldiers dragged the father off to prison and wounded the son who foolishly tried to resist. After the soldiers left, she felt a sense of dread descend on her. It settled on her chest like a dead weight, and she couldn't take a deep breath. She leaned forward just to walk. The suffocating pressure increased. It spread to her back and shoulders like a vise, pushing her into a stooped position. Each step be-came a burden. Soon she could only walk leaning on a cane for support. She walked like a feeble old woman, struggling against a heavy burden that weighed her down.

She stayed as active as she could. One thing she loved to do was come to the synagogue to hear the Scriptures read. Even though the ruler of the synagogue treated her like a cripple and tried to keep her from sitting with the rest of the women, she refused to give up coming to hear God's Word. She loved the stories of the prophets of old. Elisha and

Elijah both raised a child from the dead. They healed lepers and stood before kings and priests. Even in the Law, God promised to heal His people. She had a faint hope that maybe God still did miracles in A.D. 30.

One day she heard about a new prophet. Not long afterward, she saw Him heal people and heard Him teach in the synagogue. He was there once when the ruler tried to move her seat, and He defended her. His words had such strength and goodness about them. He said He was empowered by God to set people free, to give them the good news of new life, and touch their hearts with healing. Sometimes she thought He spoke directly to her. His words made her feel stronger and straighter on the inside. She thought about how life would be if she could be free of the weight that made her so weak and deformed.

She got there early for one Sabbath service. She hoped He would teach today as she took her seat right in the front of the women's section. When He got up to speak, He saw her. Their eyes met, and He called her up front. It took courage to leave the gallery, go down the stairs, and hobble up to meet Him, all the while leaning on her cane. But the kindness in His eyes drew her forward. She seemed to get stronger with each step. When she reached Him, He spoke gently but firmly, "From this moment on, you are free, and you are strong."

He laid His hands on her shoulders and prayed. Something powerful happened inside her chest. A light with bright rays burst open, and she felt the weight lift. She drew in a deep breath and stood up straight. Throwing her hands in the air and standing straight and tall, she praised God. She stepped forward and twirled around in a dance of freedom in front of everyone. She felt beautiful again. She stopped and looked at Him. When she saw her joy reflected in His face, she wept. His touch gave her life and freedom.

This was all too much for the ruler of the synagogue. He got up and accused the Prophet of breaking God's law by healing on the Sabbath. The Prophet defended her, calling her a daughter of Abraham and confirming her complete healing in front of everyone. He let her rejoice in her new freedom, and it became contagious. Her family and friends joined her in the front and grouped around her, praising God and singing hymns. That's when the clapping and dancing started as all the people joined in. It turned out to be a service to remember, as everyone gave the glory to God for keeping His word to His people.

———✦———

Brigette gave the glory to God when she told her story. Her new landlord offered her the possibility of holding a mortgage for her to buy the house. In the first-century Sabbath service, Jesus' healing touch restored the woman's life, and her joy spread to the whole congregation. God gave her peace and strength to replace the fear and weakness. God's word of promise prepared both of them for the good change He brought their way.

God calls us forward through His promises. His Word helps us turn our attention away from the problem and onto God, and we are ready for future change. God sees the good change in the inner man, and He rewards us openly. His love flows through our newly strengthened spirits and touches our lives.

Jesus keeps His promises to you and me today. As we keep His Word in our hearts, we are free, and we are strong.

God's Changing Room is a place where His Word lives in our hearts.

Chapter 16

Step by Step

An encounter with the living God changes us. God's creative, life-giving power comes into our inner beings. This power lives in us as new strength and health in the inner man. This godly presence, this Spirit of God, changes us into new people. Life is different because we are different.

God's resources open the way for new growth. He calls us forward to the next good and godly change. Problems and obstacles no longer stall our growth. In the life of good and godly change, there is only the next step to take, the next obstacle to overcome. God's new life is stronger than any situation you or I will ever encounter. Nothing can withstand the effects of its living power.

Even now, God's Spirit is accomplishing His life-changing work as He brings you and me to a new acceptance of His ways. God knows us better than we know ourselves. He planned a life of good and godly change, individually tailored to our needs and abilities. Step by step, God's Spirit removes the habits and attitudes that were responsible for past failures and disappointments. At the same time, He builds new godly strengths into our characters. He

114

walks with us in our new lives to help us become the spiritual men and women He created us to be.

God made this earthly realm of time and space for us. He built change into the process of life to allow us to grow, develop, and realize our potential. If it were not for this world's inherent process of change, you and I would be stuck in our present circumstances. There would be no way out, no hope, for our loved ones or for us.

God brought you and me into the world to give us an opportunity to love and serve Him, to choose the eternal over the temporal. Here is where we cooperate with the Spirit of God in our lives through good and godly change. Here is where we choose to follow the blueprint for change given in His Word. Here is where we prepare for a life of service to God in eternity.

God's power within gives us the edge we need to succeed in life's process of change. He carefully measures the flow of His power into our lives so that we move forward in a healthy, orderly pattern. Life improves on a daily basis. Our sense of satisfaction and accomplishment mounts. Our hearts open to more and more of God's power. We are living a life of which we can be proud. Our second chance at life is turning out better than we ever thought possible.

God is on our side, whether we are considering His invitation to the new life or are already walking in a right relationship with Him. He turns no one away. God already wiped the slate clean of the past. The future rests in the hands of a loving heavenly Father. Today God loves us, and we love Him in return. We appreciate what we have today and look forward to tomorrow. Today God's Spirit removes more weakness and builds more strength. Today we follow God's Word as closely as we can. Tomorrow we improve some more.

God is so committed to our success that He laid down His life to make it all possible. He calls you and me by His love into the life of good and godly change. His power touches each and every one of us. Step by step we grow and change.

We receive God's strength for today and live in hope for tomorrow. Good things are always on the way.

About the Author

Linn DeGennaro co-pastors According to the Way of Christ Jesus Ministries with her husband, Jim. The ministry encourages others with the Word of God through a newsletter, online devotional and one-on-one ministry. Linn and Jim reside in New Jersey and are available for speaking engagements.

To contact the author for speaking engagements:

linndegennaro975@hotmail.com
or contact
According to the Way of Christ Jesus Ministries at
133 Fredon-Marksboro Rd.
Newton, NJ 07860